SIGN WITH US

by Teresa Lacy Castle and Dan J. Castle

FOR ALL AGES — EASY TO LEARN

Dedication

To our loving daughters, Nicole and Brittany who gave us the inspiration to create this book.

This book is dedicated to our daughters, their friends, and all the people who want to learn sign language.

Photos

Most of the photos were taken by Teresa Lacy Castle and Dan J. Castle
The girls in the photos are Nicole and Brittany Castle.

Table of Contents

Getting Started with American Sign Language

Over twenty-two million Americans are hearing-impaired. American Sign Language (ASL) is the fourth most used language in the United States. **ASL is a fun and beautiful language to learn.** Sign language is seen more and more on television, movies, elementary classrooms, and in college courses.

ASL is a very visual language and the signs may represent ideas, concepts, things, actions, or a string of ideas. Many Deaf people see the pictures or movies of the actual objects in their mind while they are signing, just as some people hear the words in their minds when they are thinking.

This book is meant for all ages. For hearing, hard-of-hearing and deaf people, children or adults. This book will help you learn sign language.

How to use this book

The signs are grouped by topics: the Alphabet, Numbers, Opposites, Animals, Foods, Colors and More Signs. The vocabulary is shown through photographs of the signs by children. The photographs of the signs have arrows on them indicating the direction of movement. A description in English below the picture helps you with the movement, direction, location and origination of the signs.

As in many languages the structures are similar to other languages. In the case of ASL, the structures of time indicators instead of verb tense is similar to the Hopi language. The fact that the signs represent pictures and not sounds or letters is similar to the Japanese and Chinese languages. The fact that

the descriptive words are after the noun instead of the before is similar to many romance languages much as Spanish or French.

You will find the manual alphabet and numbers in the front section of this book for quick reference. Also you can refer to the index at the back of the book for a listing of all the signs in the book by page number. The practice section is after the vocabulary section for you to practice the vocabulary in sentences.

Facial Expression

The importance of facial expression cannot be understated. As you can see the children signing in the book many of the pictures have very expressive faces.

The face plays an important role in signing. If you have had friends from other countries maybe you have noticed that some people use their hands more than others. And some people use their facial expressions more than others. In ASL the facial expression not only adds to the sign and the meaning but asking questions as well.

Fingerspelling

Fingerspelling is the representation of the alphabet on the hands. It is sometimes called the Manual Alphabet. It is not sign language but a representation of English. As some words become used over time some fingerspelled words become adopted into sign language such as gas, apt, job and car. When fingerspelled in a special way they represent a "loan sign" and not the fingerspelled word but the object it is referring to. Also you fingerspell words that have no sign like people's names and places.

Fingerspelling Rules

• Fingerspelling a word that you don't know how to sign is very acceptable.

• Keep the fingers moving smoothly. Keep your fingerspelling crisp and smooth.

• Don't bounce your hand. Keep it steady and in one place.

• Pause between words. The pause is normally a second or two in length.

Arrows

Sometimes the arrows are meant to move straight out and not to the side. Be sure to read the description below the sign to make sure.

Dominant Hand

Be sure to use the dominant hand (or your favorite hand) to sign all the signs. The main hand doing the action is your dominant hand.

Example: OUT

The description under the sign for OUT says...

similar to in but in the opposite direction use the in sign and move the hand out of the o-shaped hand as if taking it out of the other hand

The **o-shaped hand is the dominant hand** and the other hand means your non-dominant hand. So if you are left-handed do the **letter o** with your left hand. If you are right-handed do the **letter o** with your right hand.

Pointing

Pointing is signing. Most times pointing indicates an object or person. Sometimes it means IT. Dan would say in his sign language classes,

"If you can point to it, you can sign it."

If an object or person is in viewing range and the other person can recognize what you are pointing at, pointing is a great way of signing it, he, she or something that is seen by both persons. If I was in a room and saw 100 items, I could point to each and the other person would understand. For example, if I pointed to a computer that would be the sign IT (computer). In a sentence I might sign,

IT ME LIKE	I like the **computer**.
IT BROKEN	It is broken.

IT is referring to the object that is being pointed at.

Plurals

In English an s is usually added to indicate a plural, in ASL a plural is indicated in different ways. One way is to sign MANY after the object, as DOG MANY. Another way is to indicate how many such as DOG TWO. Another way is to sign the object twice such as HOUSE HOUSE, indicating two houses. There are many other ways to indicate plurals just as English has many ways.

Eye Contact

Be sure to make eye contact with the person you are signing to. Looking away while signing is considered to be impolite.

Regionalization or Dialects

As in most languages there are dialects. In American Sign Language sometimes there may be only one sign used nationwide or many variations of the sign. Remember to be flexible and accepting of different styles and ways of signing.

Practice

- Practice signing and fingerspelling everyday.
- Find someone to practice with. That makes it easier and more fun, especially having someone to sign to.

Finally...

We hope you enjoy this book as much as we had fun putting this book together. Have fun and maybe learn with a friend or teach your children.

If you want more information or more courses on ASL contact your local adult education program, community college or the Deaf Community agencies in your area. This will help increase your vocabulary and improve your signing skills.

Happy Signing,

Teresa Lacy Castle
Dan J. Castle
Nicole and Brittany

Basic Hand Shapes

bent flat hand

curved fingers

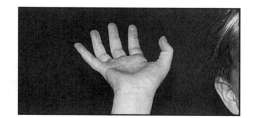

claw hand

flat hand up

flat hand down

flat o

index finger

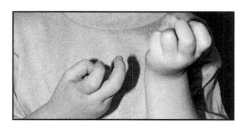

double x

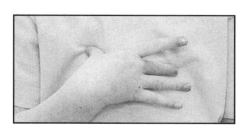

open 8

The pictures above represent basic hands shapes that are not already represented by number and alphabet shapes.

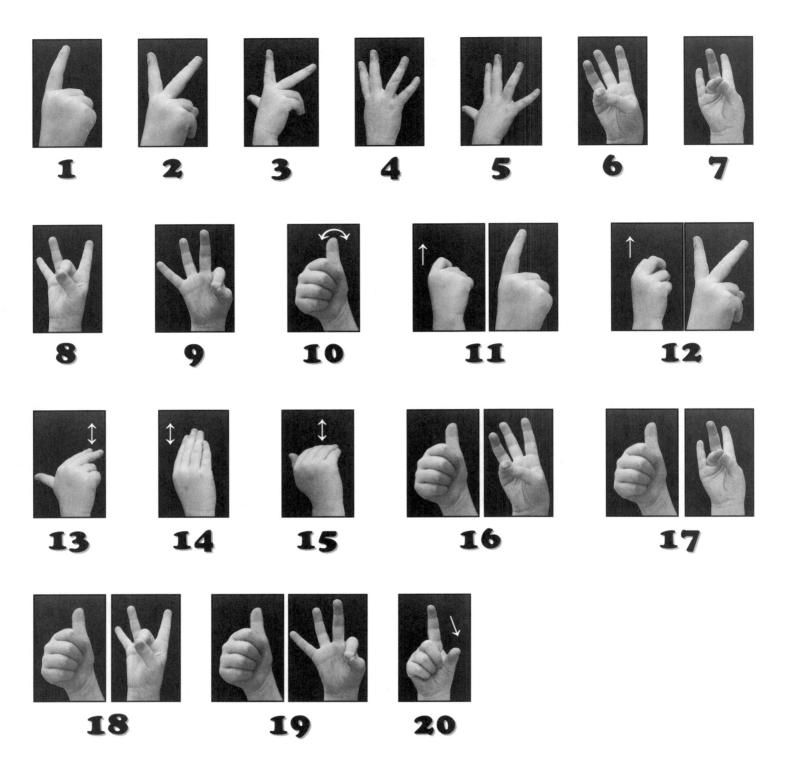

The Numbers
1 - 20

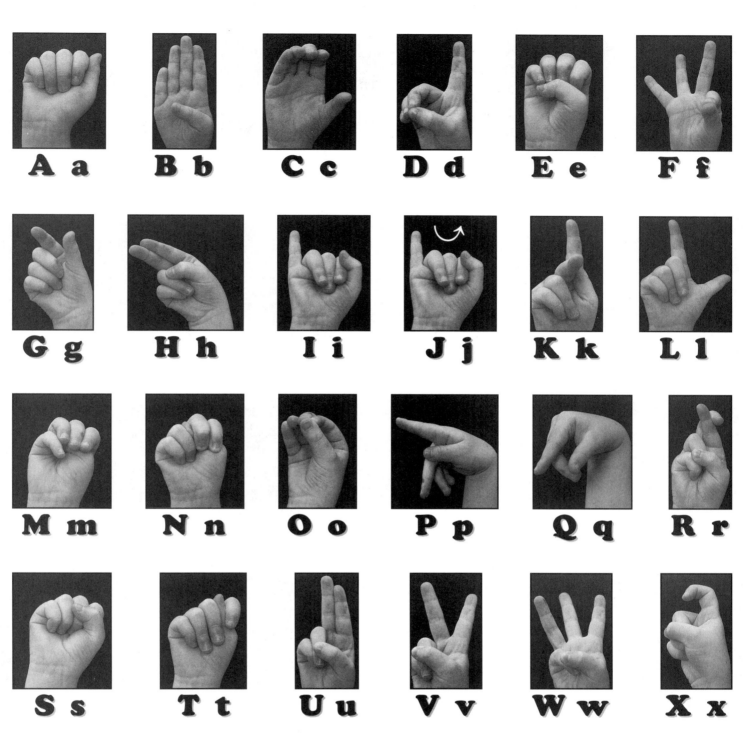

A a   B b   C c   D d   E e   F f

G g   H h   I i   J j   K k   L l

M m   N n   O o   P p   Q q   R r

S s   T t   U u   V v   W w   X x

Y y   Z z

The Manual Alphabet

7

Alphabet

fingerspelling

with 5-shaped hand palm down and in front of body
wiggle the fingers several times and move
hand to the right

a b c d e f g h i j k l m

n o p q r s t u v w x y z

A a

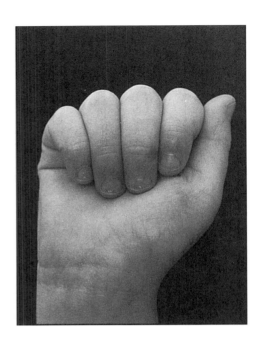

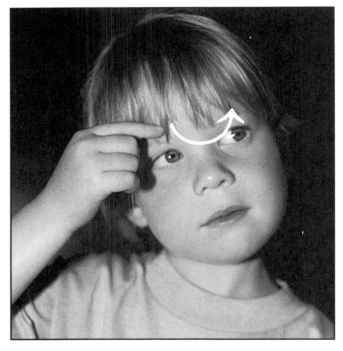

place index finger on forehead then
move out while curving upward slightly

A   is   for

airplane

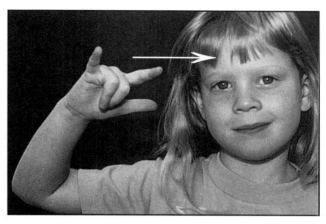

use the y-shaped (or "I love you" hand shape) with index finger extended and move in the air as a plane forward twice

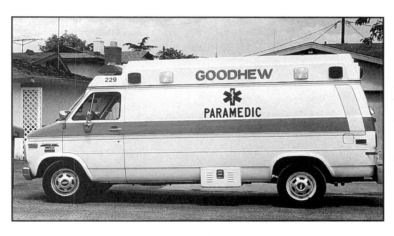

ambulance

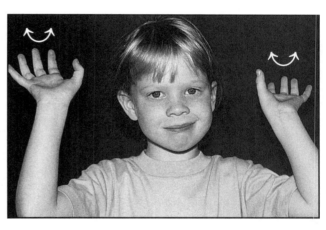

use the claw hand shape and twist wrists back and forth several times as if indicating the moving lights on top

apron

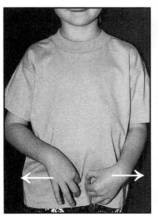

use the f-shape hands and touch waist in front then move hands to opposite hips as if putting on an apron

B b

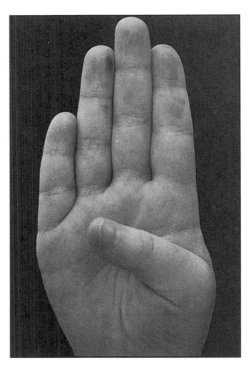

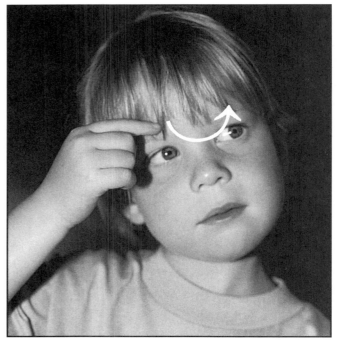

place index finger on forehead then
move out while curving upward slightly

B is for

bath

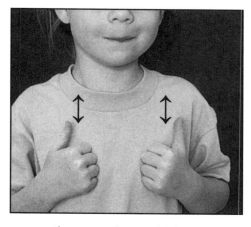

use the ten-shaped hand with thumbs up and knuckles on chest move hands up and down at the same time as if bathing

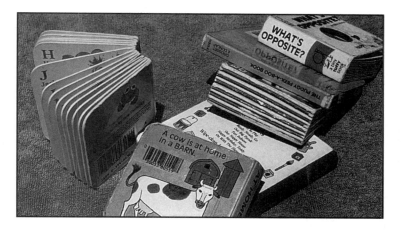

book

use the flat hands held together palms to each other open the hands as if opening a book

box

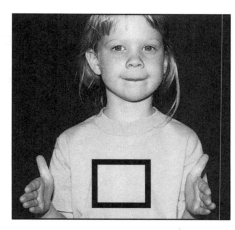

use the flat hands opposite each other by making opposites sides, left right then top and bottom sides

A B C

C c

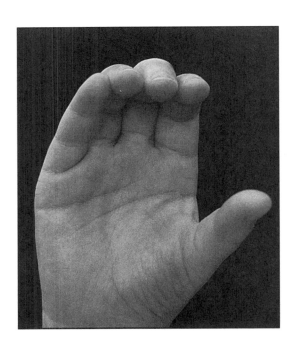

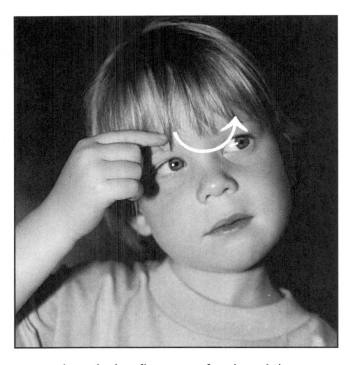

place index finger on forehead then
move out while curving upward slightly

C   is   for

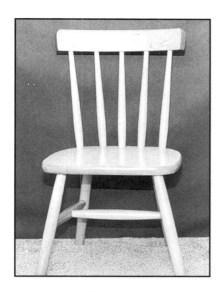

chair

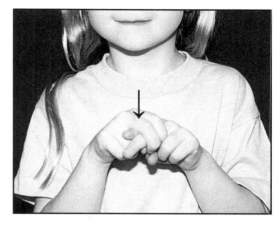

use the u-shaped hands and put
one on top of the other twice
as if sitting

clock

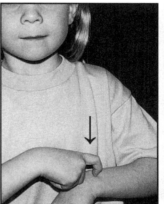 

use the time sign (x-shape hand placed on
left wrist once) then use two c-shaped
hands and place in front of face
as if putting a clock on the wall

cup

use the c-shaped hand on top of flat
left hand as if putting a cup on the
hand

14

A B C D

D d

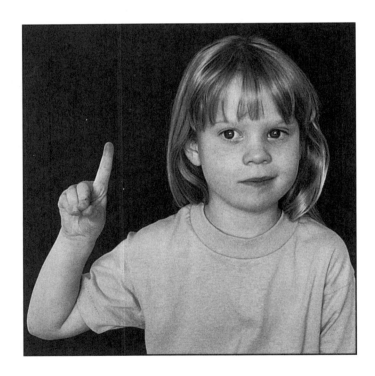

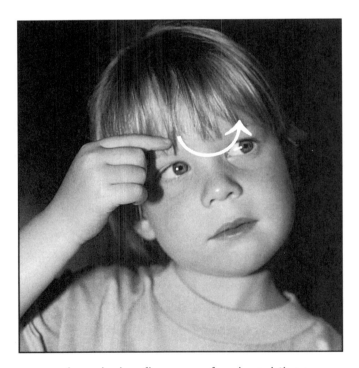

place index finger on forehead then
move out while curving upward slightly

D   is   for

dinosaur

use the d-shaped and moving to the left and bounce it several times as if a dinosaur was moving

doll

use the x-shaped hand on nose and bring down to tip several times

drum

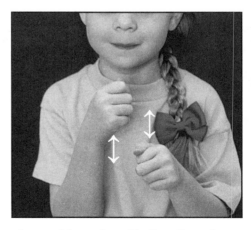

use the x-shaped hands with the thumb touching index fingers as if holding drum sticks and move up and down several times

16

E e

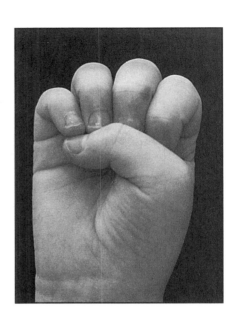

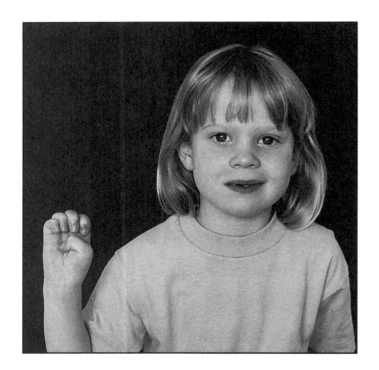

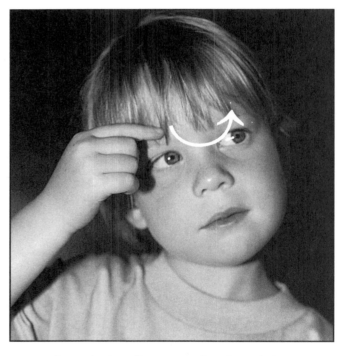

place index finger on forehead then
move out while curving upward slightly

E   is   for

17

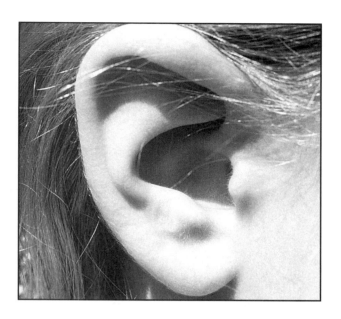

ear

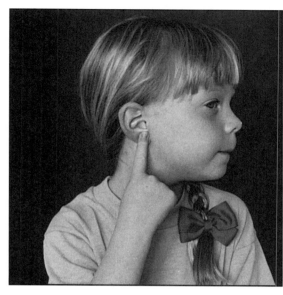

use the index finger and touch the ear

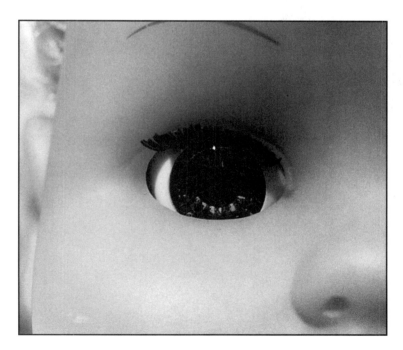

eye

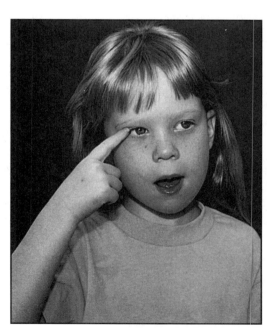

use the index finger and point to the eye or touch right below the eye

18

A B C D E F

F f

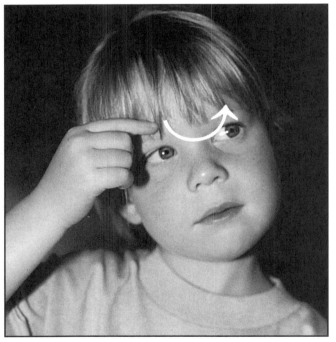

place index finger on forehead then
move out while curving upward slightly

F   is   for

19

fence

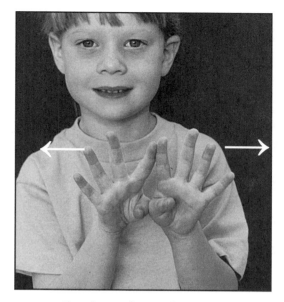

use the four-shaped hands with palms facing outward and move both in opposite directions as if showing the boards of a fence

flag

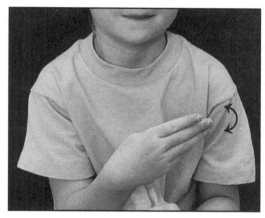

use the index pointing up on the left hand and place the wrist of the right hand in front of and touching the index finger and shake the b-shaped hand back and forth several times as if a flag is waving

fork

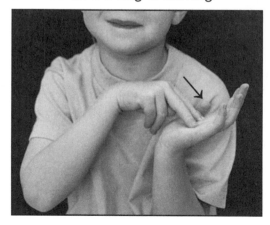

use the two or w-shaped hand and put tips on other hand two times as if a fork was touching the hand

20

G g

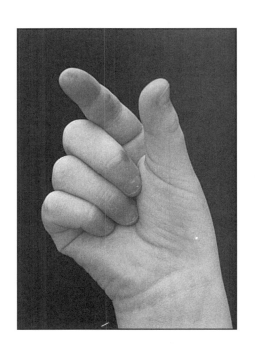

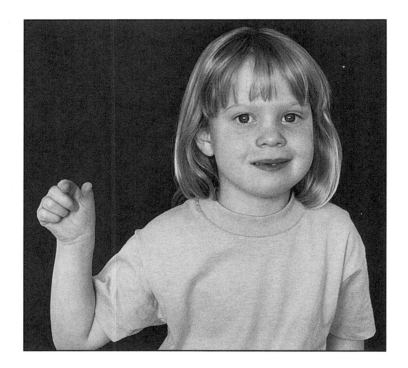

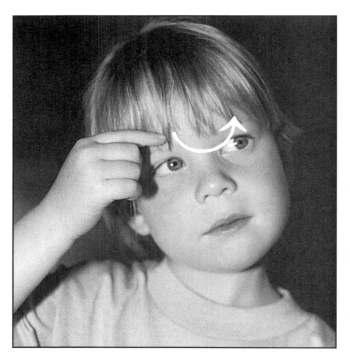

place index finger on forehead then
move out while curving upward slightly

G is for

game

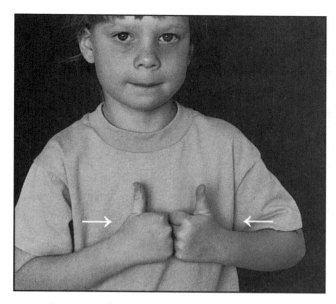

use the ten-shaped hand with knuckles facing each other and several inches apart bring the knucles together two times

glasses

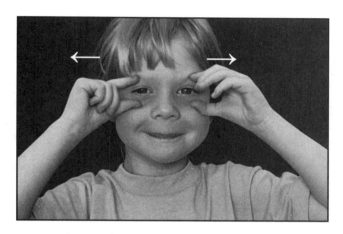

use the g-shaped hands and place near eyes and then close thumb and index fingers as moving hands out two inches as if showing the frames of the glasses

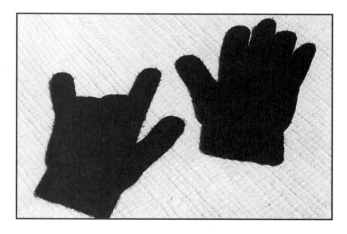

glove

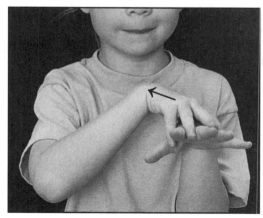

use the five-shaped hand palms down and place on top of the other hand then draw back the top hand as if putting on a glove

22

A B C D E F G H

H h

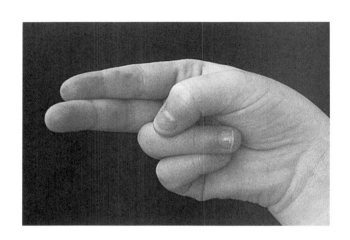

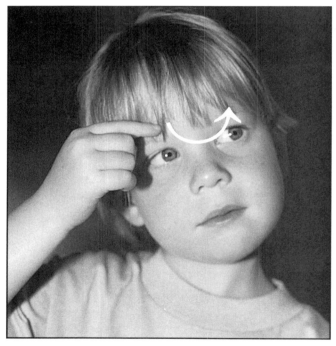

place index finger on forehead then
move out while curving upward slightly

H   is   for

23

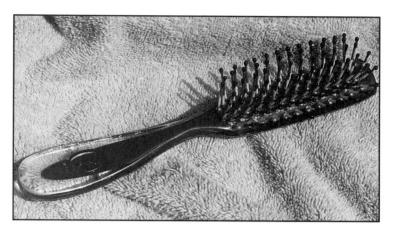

hairbrush

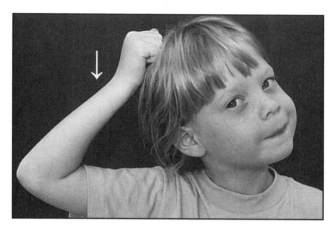

use the a-shaped hand brush against hair two times as if brushing the hair

hammer

use the s-shaped hand as if holding a hammer and move outward and downward two times as if hitting a nail

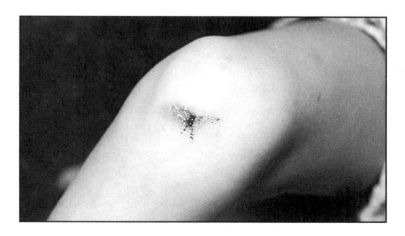

hurt

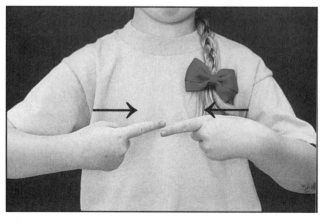

use the index fingers holding them two inches apart and while twisting fingers in an opposite direction bring inward an inch

I i

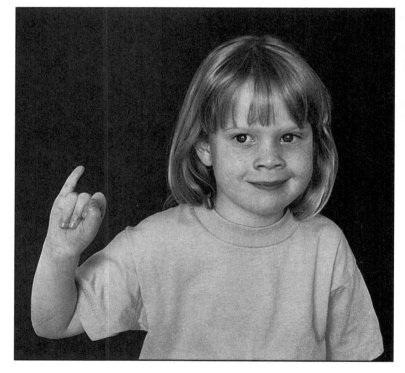

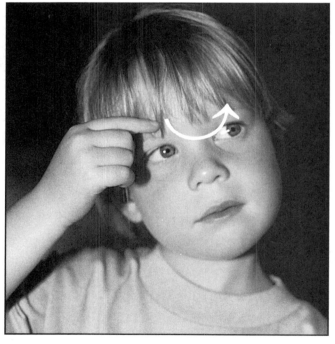

place index finger on forehead then
move out while curving upward slightly

I   is   for

ice

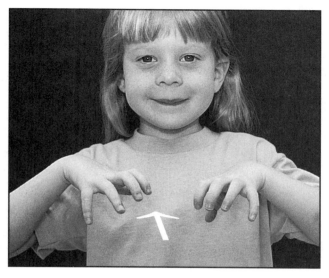

first sign water - then use the two 5-shaped hands and move inward while turning hands into claw shapes

Indian

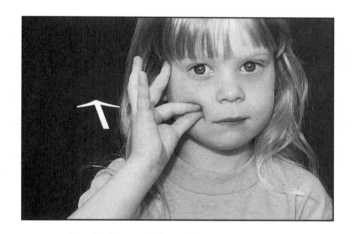

use the f-shaped hand and tap on cheek
and tap again near ear once
(as if painting your face)

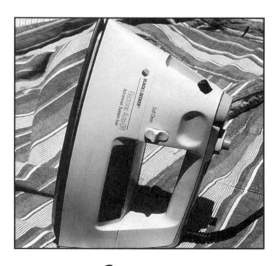

iron

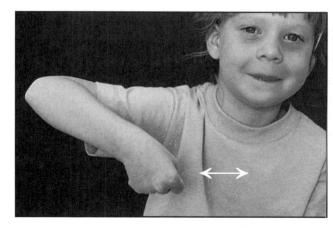

use the s-shaped hand as if holding
an iron and move to the left two times
as if carrying ironing

A B C D E F G H I J

J j

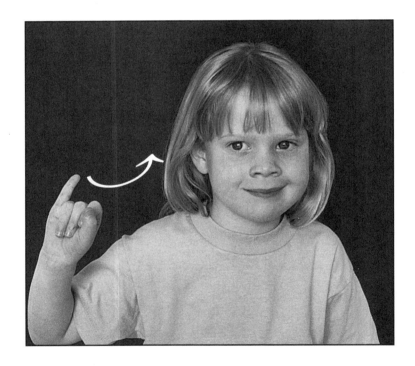

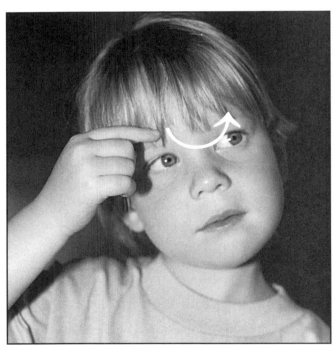

place index finger on forehead then
move out while curving upward slightly

J   is   for

jacket

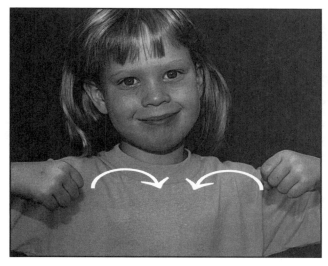

use the ten-shaped hand with thumbs
touching just below shoulders and move
down to center of chest
as if putting on a jacket

jelly

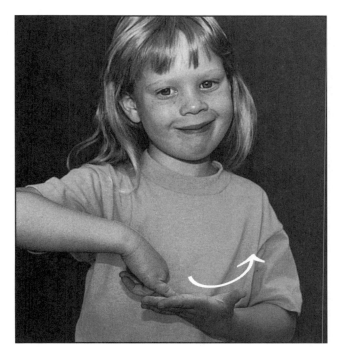

use the j-shaped hand on flat palm up and
draw the bottom part of the j on the hand
as if scooping up some jelly

A B C D E F G H I J K

K k

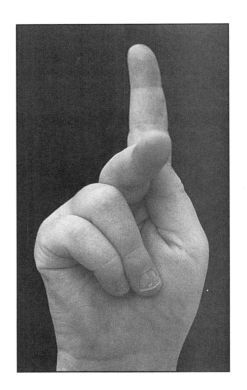

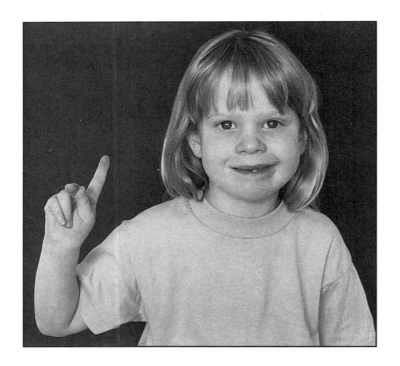

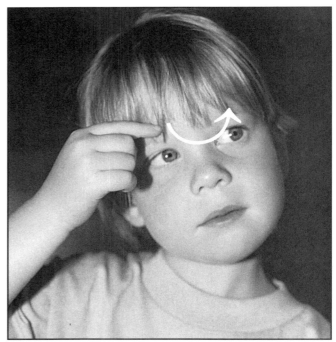

place index finger on forehead then
move out while curving upward slightly

K is for

29

king

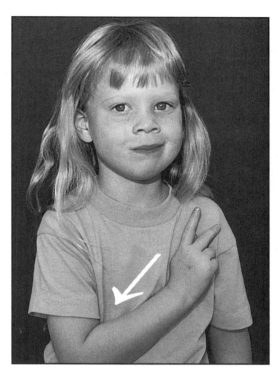

use the k-shaped hand with the
thumb on the shoulder and move
hand down across chest to opposite
hip as if showing the royal sash

kitchen

use the k-shaped hand with thumb touching
the flat hand and flip k over so back of hand
is touching palm as if flipping over pancakes

A B C D E F G H I J K L

L l

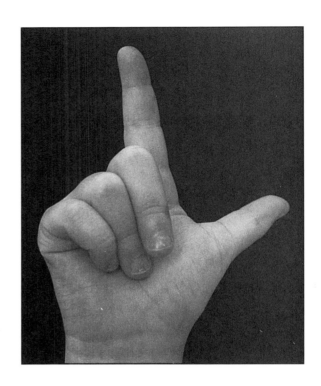

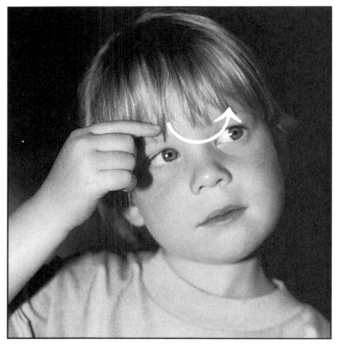

place index finger on forehead then
move out while curving upward slightly

L   is   for

31

lamp

use the flat o-shaped hand held up above
shoulder and open hand
as if showing the light is on

leaf

use the flat open hand with palm down and
move the hand downward and left and right
as if a leaf was floating downward

luggage

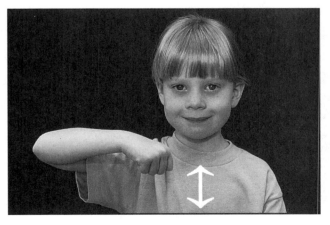

use the s-shaped hand and move up and
down as if carrying luggage (same as bucket)

M m

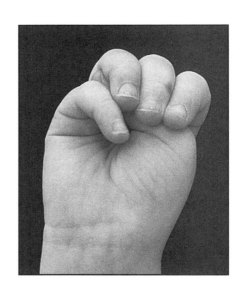

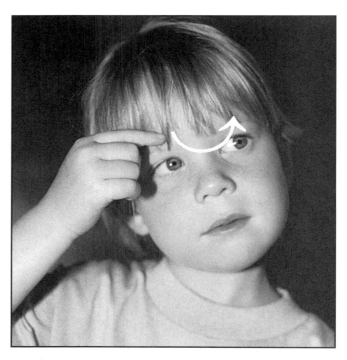

place index finger on forehead then
move out while curving upward slightly

M is for

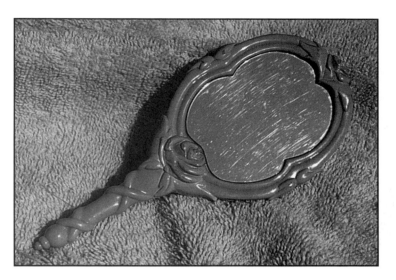

mirror

use the flat hand with palm facing you and
wiggle back and forth several times
as if looking in a mirror

money

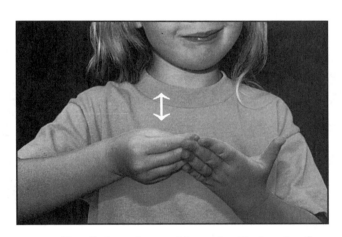

use the flat o-shaped hand with back of
hand on top of flat palm hand and move up
and down two times
as if holding paper money

mop

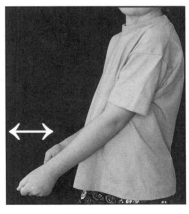

use the x-shaped hand with thumb tucked
under x hook and move back and forth
as if holding a mop and mopping

34

N n

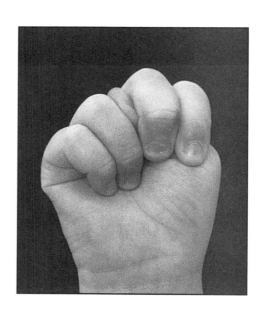

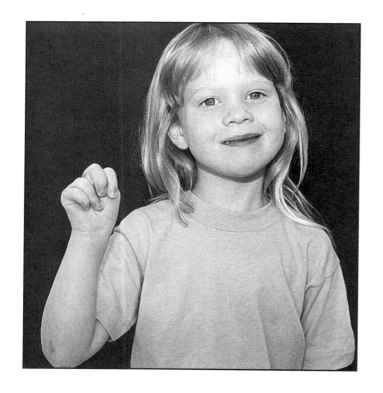

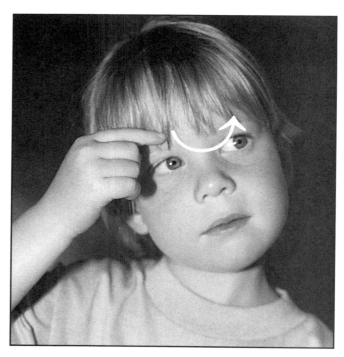

place index finger on forehead then
move out while curving upward slightly

N is for

napkin

use the flat b-hand with palm near mouth
move in circular or patting motion
as if holding and using a napkin

necklace

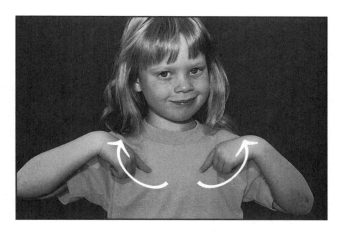

use the index fingers move from front to
rear of the neck as if pointing where the
necklace would be

newspaper

print: use the beginning of the sign for twenty (thumb and index finger apart) with back of thumb touching
flat palm up of other hand and touch index onto thumb two times as if printing ink onto the page

paper: use two flat palms with one above the other then push the top hand onto the other hand two times
as if paper was going through a machine

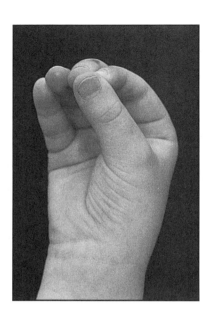

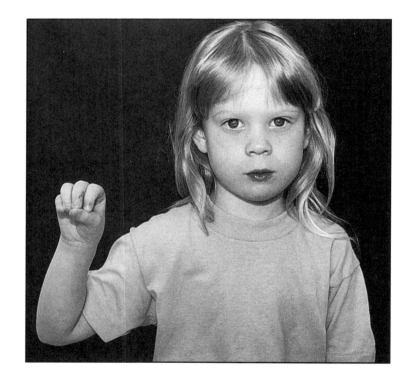 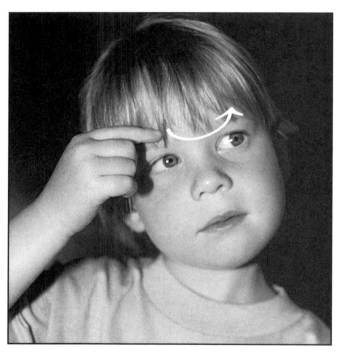

place index finger on forehead then
move out while curving upward slightly

O is for

ocean

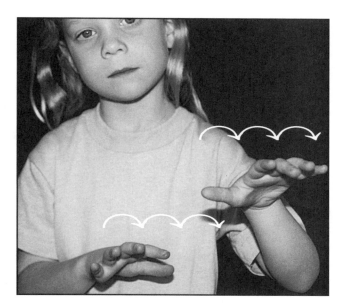

sign water first: w-shaped hand on lips two times
wave: use the flat 5-hands with palms down and move outward and in wavy motion as if showing the waves

oven

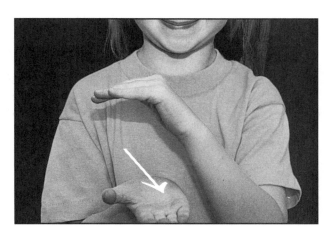

with the bent-hand shape on the left hand show the top of the oven, with the right flat hand palm up move it forward under the other hand (as if putting something into the oven)

P p

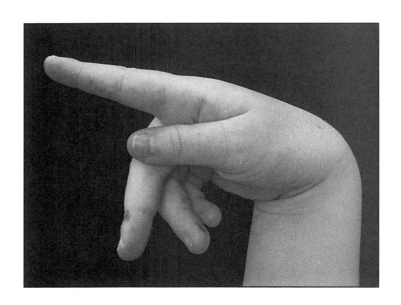

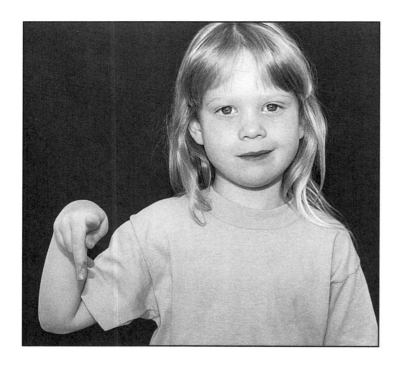

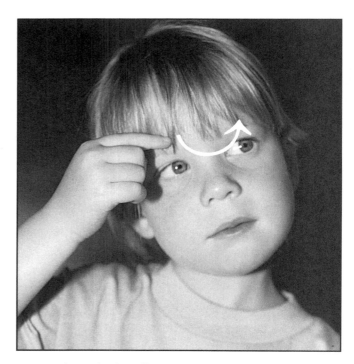

place index finger on forehead then
move out while curving upward slightly

P   is   for

pencil

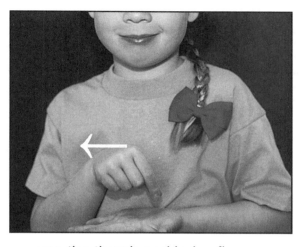

use the thumb and index fingers together as if holding a pencil and slide across the other hand's palm as if writing

plant

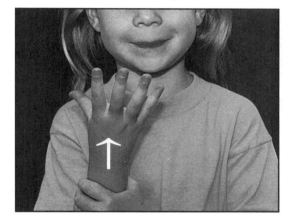

use the flat o-shaped hand and with the left hand wrap it around the other hand and push the right hand upwards as if a plant was growing

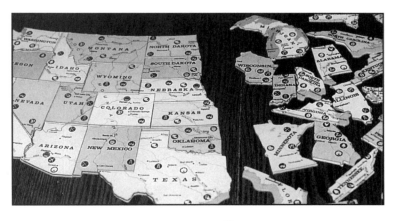

puzzle

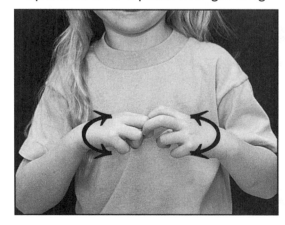

use the double x-shaped hands and rub the knucles against each other and twist wrists with opposite clockwise and counter-clockwise motion

Q q

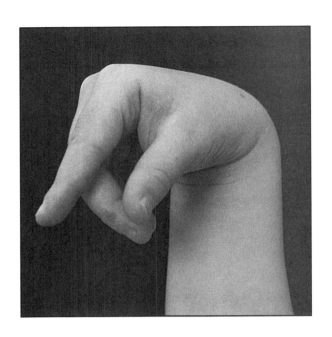

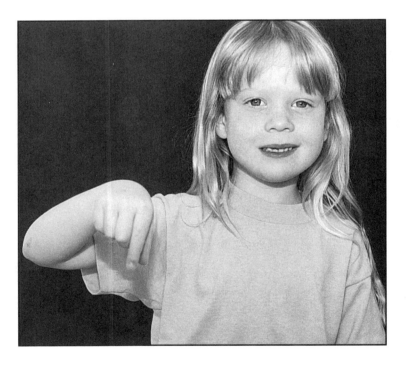

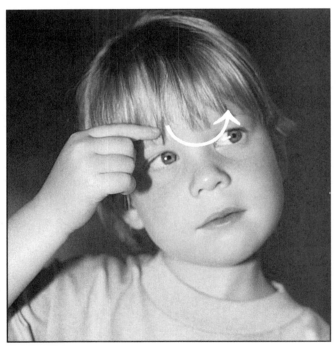

place index finger on forehead then
move out while curving upward slightly

Q is for

queen

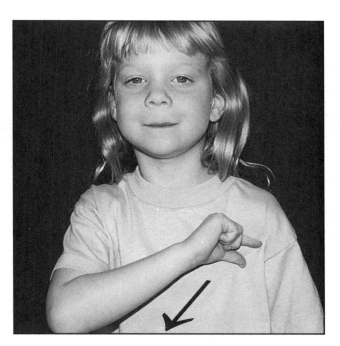

use the q-shaped hand with the thumb on
the shoulder pointed down, move hand
down across chest to opposite hip
as if tracing the royal sash

quilt

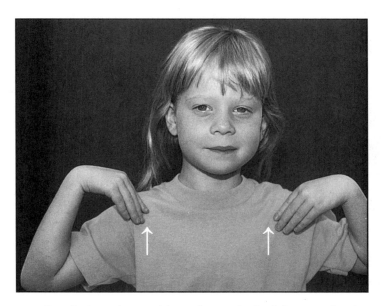

use the flat o-shaped hands and start from a foot
out in front of the waist and pull back to shoulders
as if pulling a quilt onto oneself

A B C D E F G H I J K L M

R r

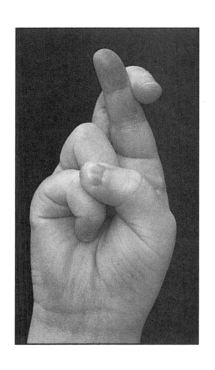

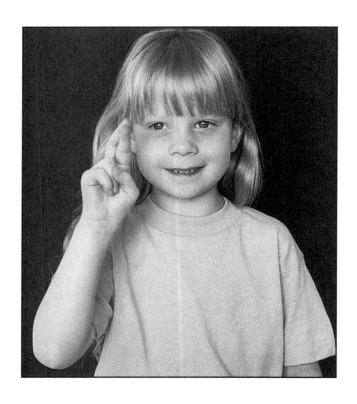

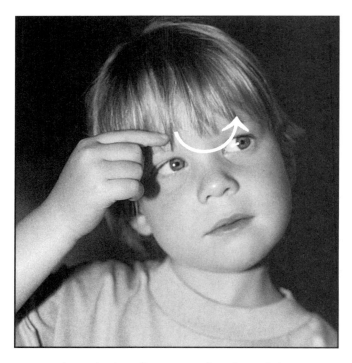

place index finger on forehead then
move out while curving upward slightly

R   is   for

43

rainbow

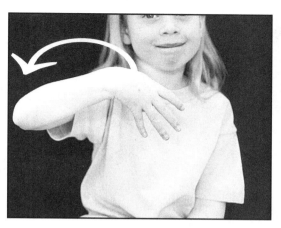

use the four shaped hand and move
out to the right as if tracing a rainbow

ring

use the thumb and index finger and place
on either side of the ring finger and move
downward towards hand as if placing a
ring on the finger

rock

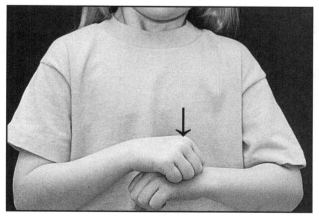

use two s-shaped hands and knock one
knuckle on the other knuckle two times
as if hitting a rock onto another rock

A B C D E F G H I J K L M

S s

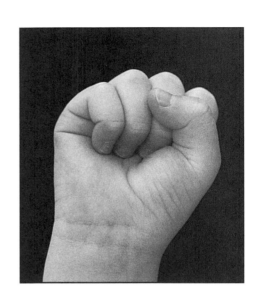

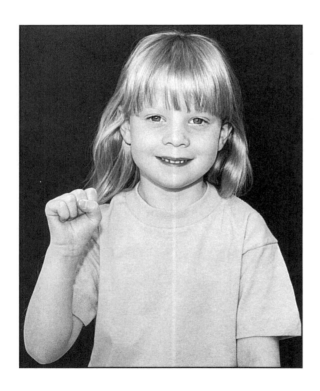

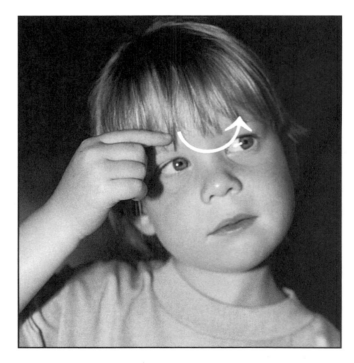

place index finger on forehead then
move out while curving upward slightly

S   is   for

Scissors

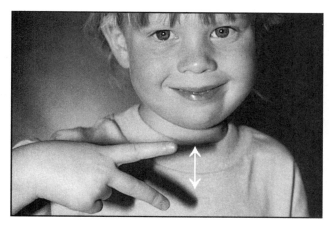

use the two-shaped hand and move fingers together two times as if cutting paper

Skates

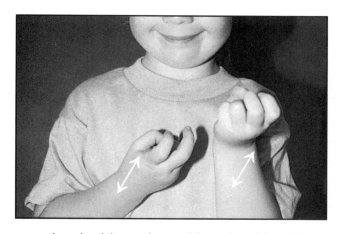

use the double x-shaped hands with palms up and move both hands forwards to the left and then forwards to the right gracefully several times as if rollerskating

Socks

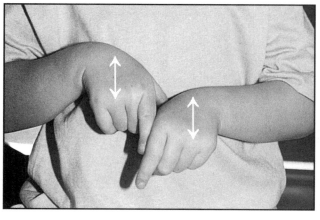

use the two index fingers and with sides of fingers touching move back and forth as if knitting socks

T t

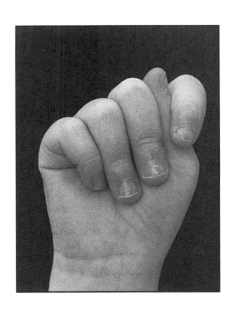

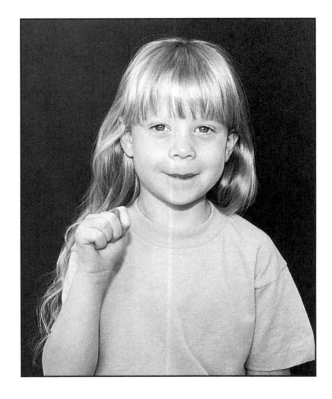

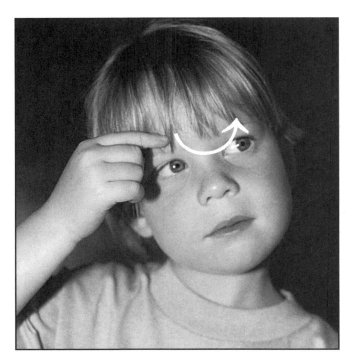

place index finger on forehead then
move out while curving upward slightly

T is for

table

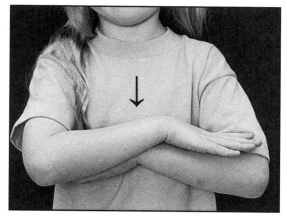

place the two arms one on top of the
other as if showing the table top

telephone

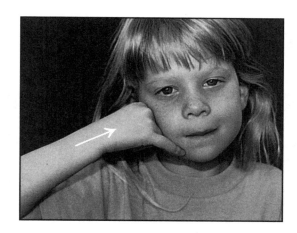

use the y-shaped hand and place
up to the ear and mouth with thumb
near ear as if using the phone

toilet

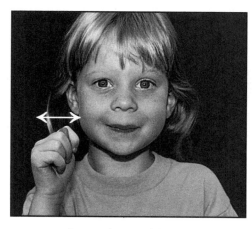

use the t-shaped hand and
move back and forth as if pacing
waiting for the bathroom

48

U u

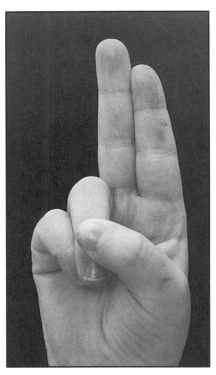

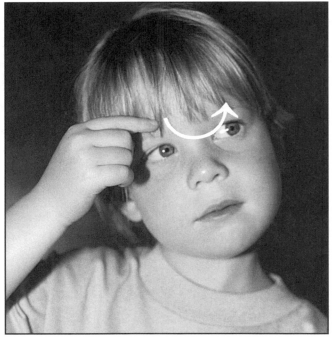

place index finger on forehead then
move out while curving upward slightly

U   is   for

umbrella

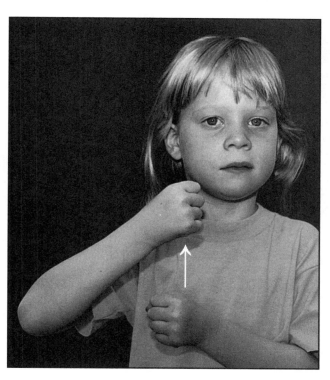

use the two s-shaped hands one on top of the other as if holding an umbrella then move the right hand up as if opening up the umbrella

unicorn

use the index finger and place wrist on forehead with index finger pointing out as if showing the horn of the unicorn

50

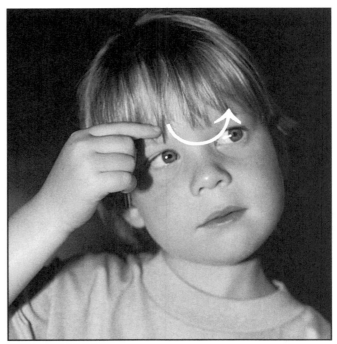

place index finger on forehead then
move out while curving upward slightly

v is for

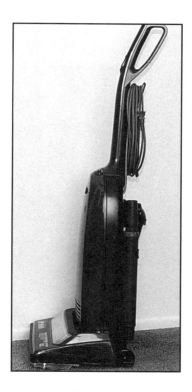

vacuum

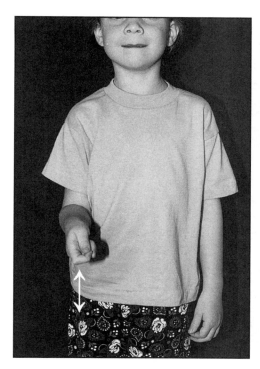

use the thumb-in-x-shaped hand
and move back and forth
as if pushing and pulling
a vacuum

vase

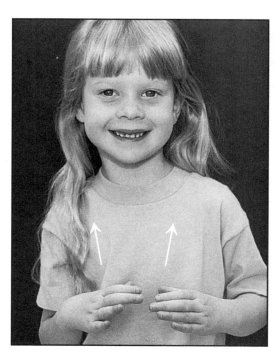

use the c-shaped hands and move
them upwards as if showing the
sides of a vase

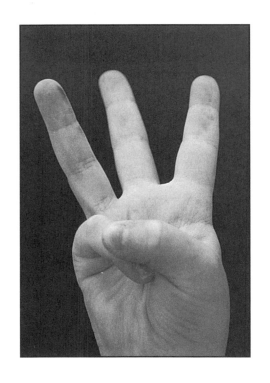

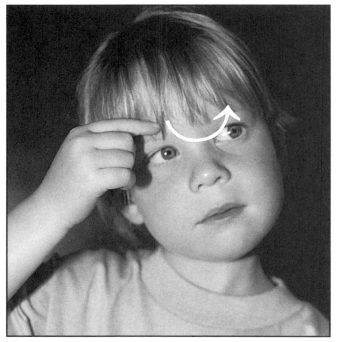

place index finger on forehead then
move out while curving upward slightly

W   **is**   **for**

watch

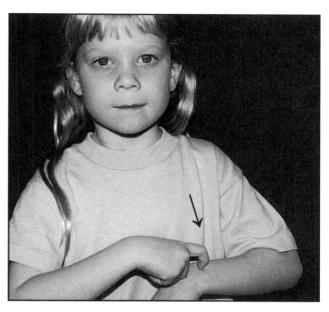

use the x-shaped hand and place on wrist
of other hand with palm down as if
pointing to the watch
(also used for the sign for time)

whale

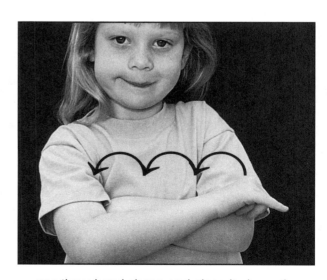

use the y-hand shape and place it above the
elbow of the other arm and pull the y back across
the arm in a wavy motion as if showing the movement of a whale's tail moving in water

A B C D E F G H I J K L M

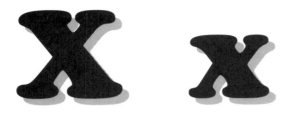

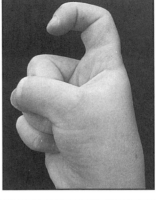

X **x**

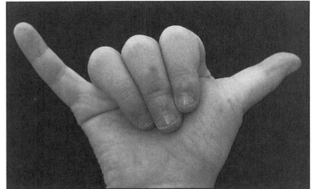

Y **y**

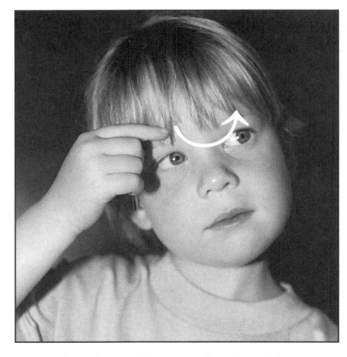

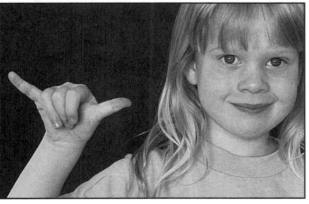

place index finger on forehead then
move out while curving upward slightly

X Y are for

xylophone

use the thumb-in-x-shaped hand and move up and down as if holding sticks and hitting a xylophone

yarn

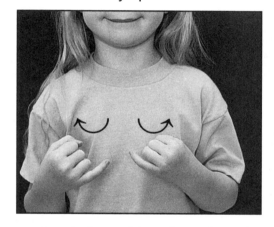

use two i-shaped hands and touch the little finger tips and move outward in a circular motion two times as if pulling string

yo-yo

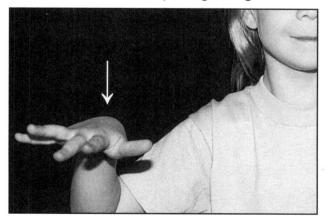

use the five-hand shape with palm down and move hand up and down as if using a yo-yo

A B C D E F G H I J K L M

Z z

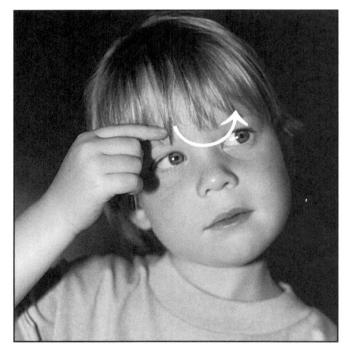

place index finger on forehead then
move out while curving upward slightly

Z   is   for

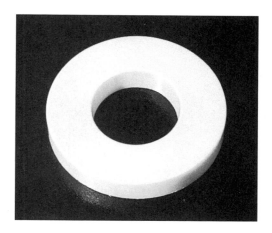

zero

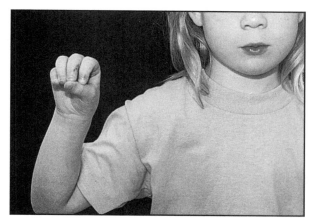

use the o-shaped hand and hold it out in front of the body as if showing a zero

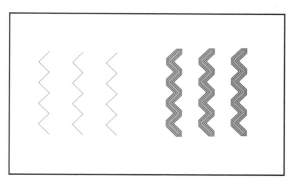

zig zag

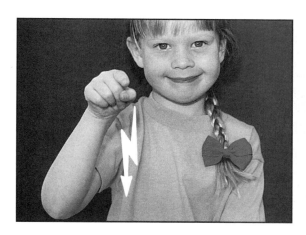

use the index finger and move the finger down in a zig-zag motion

zipper

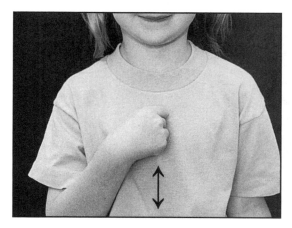

use the thumb-in-x-shaped hand shape and move up and down on chest as if using a zipper

Foods

pretend to eat food
use flat o-shaped hand move it
twice to the mouth

Apple

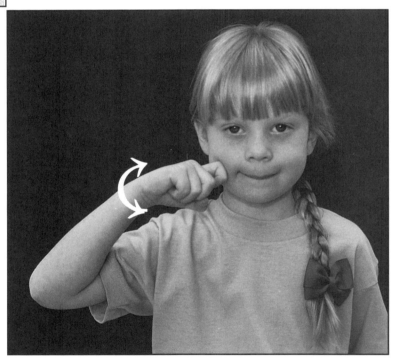

put x-shaped hand on cheek and twist two times

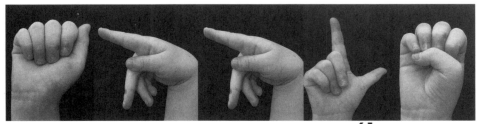

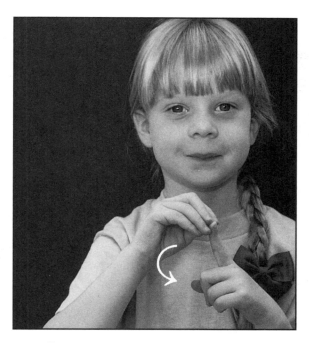

put flat-o shaped hand on index finger
of non-dominant hand
move down several times
pretend to pull banana peels off

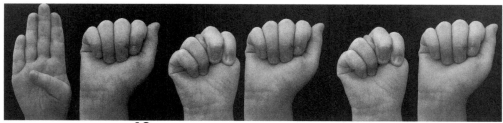

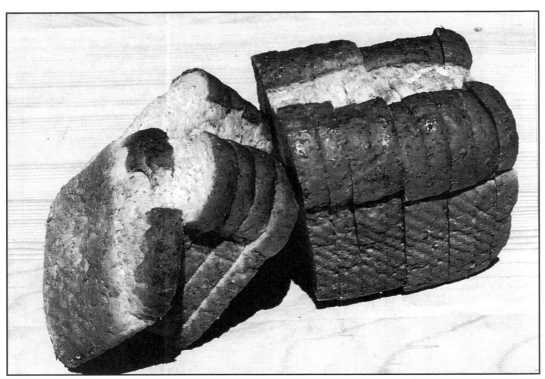

Bread

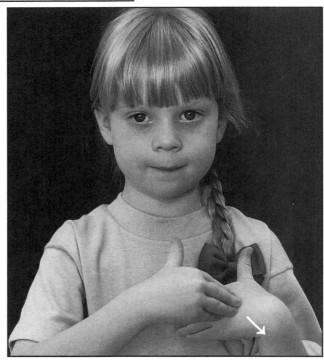

Stroke hand on top of other two times
using a bent- flat hand
pretend to cut bread slices

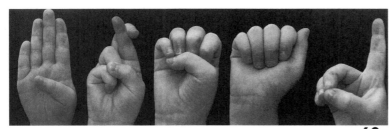

63

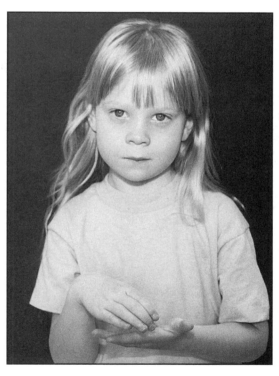

Cake

pretend to cut cake using a c-shaped
hand make an x on the hand as if
showing the cut of the cake into
squares the fingertips touching the
palm of the
non-dominant (or opposite) hand

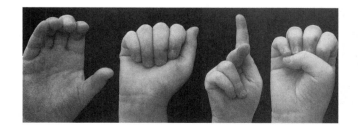

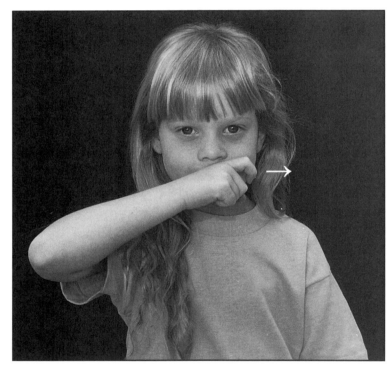

using an x-shaped hand wiggle the index finger
while moving the hand across the face toward the
non-dominant side

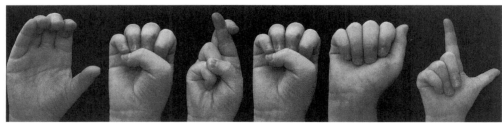

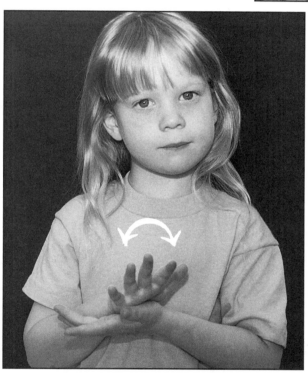

pretend to be pressing cheese
between palms
twist the top flat hand on top of the other
several times

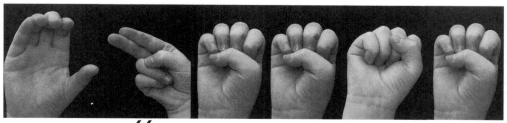

Cookie

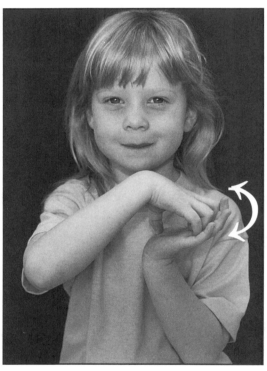

pretend to show shape of cookie
in palm using claw-shaped hand
place fingertips on opposite palm
and then twist hand and touch
other palm again

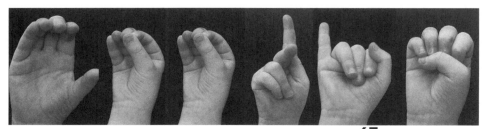

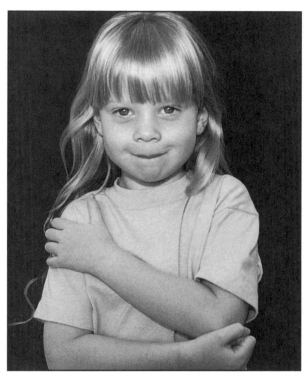

using a s-shaped hand bounce it on the
elbow of the other arm twice
(the left hand should be a s-shape hand
on the shoulder or in the air)

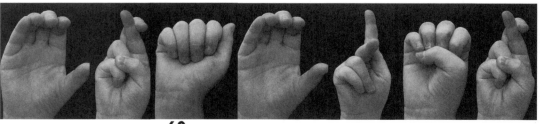

French Fries

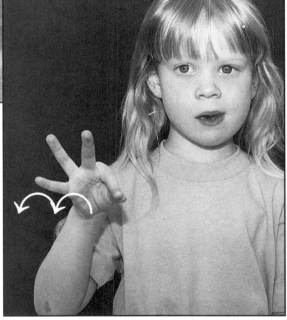

using the f-shaped hand move it towards the opposite side of the body in a bouncy motion two times (as if to show the first two letters of the food or to show the length of the fry)

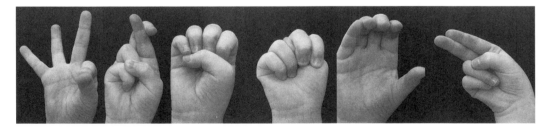

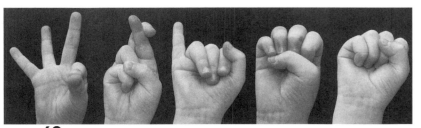

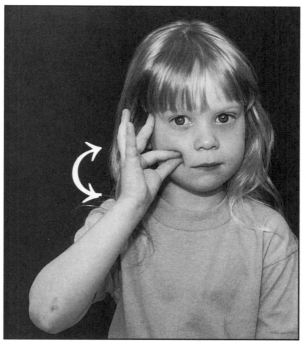

twist f-shaped hand on cheek
several times (newer sign)

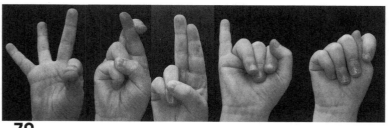

Ice Cream

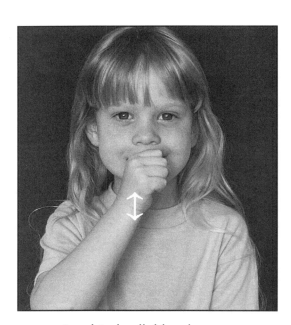

pretend to be licking ice cream from a cone, hold hand in a s-shaped hand and bring down from mouth two times

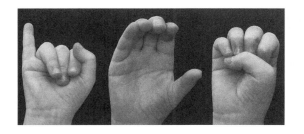

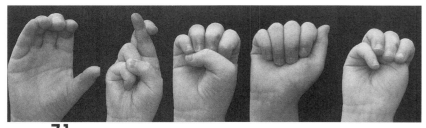

Hamburger

hold both hands together as if to form a hamburger patty
then disconnect hands and reform them together but with
opposite hand on top this time

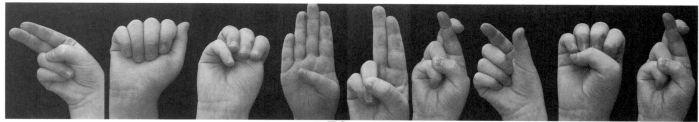

Meat

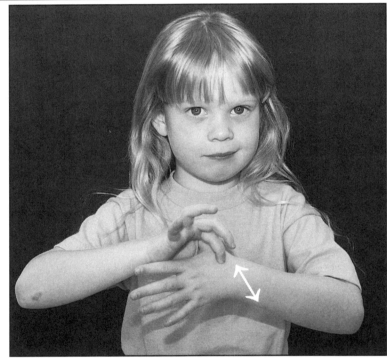

with the thumb and index finger grab the loose skin
from the other hand and move both hands together
up and down two times
as if showing a slice of meat

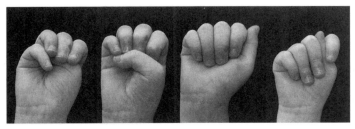

pretend to milk a cow with one hand
using a s-shaped hand squeeze and unsqueeze
two times

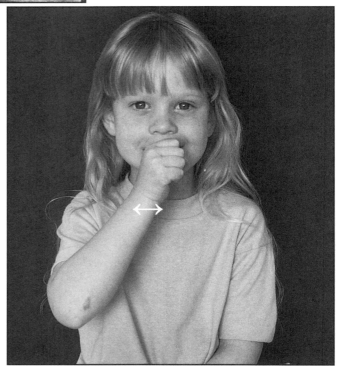

Orange

pretend to squeeze orange juice in mouth from an orange, using a s-shaped hand- squeeze hand two times on mouth

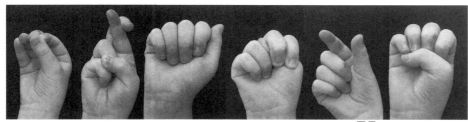

Peanut
Butter

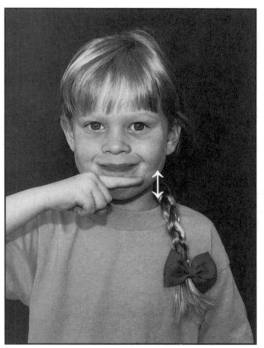

with index finger anchored to the
chin twist the finger two times

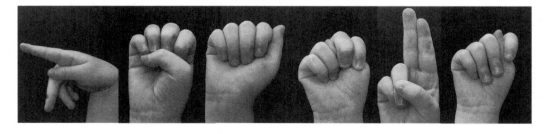

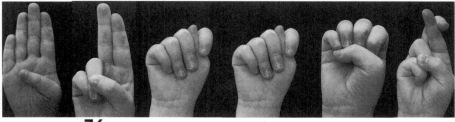

Pizza

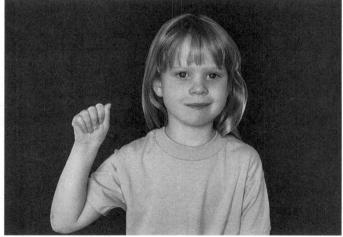

using a two-shaped hand actually forming the beginnings of two z's
move two fingers in the shape of a z and end up with making an a-shaped hand
(spelling the last three letters of pizza, z-z-a)

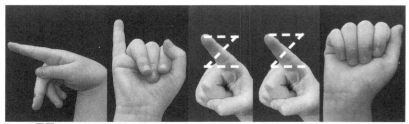

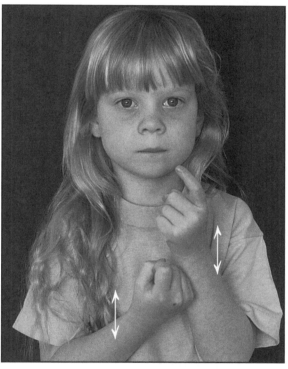

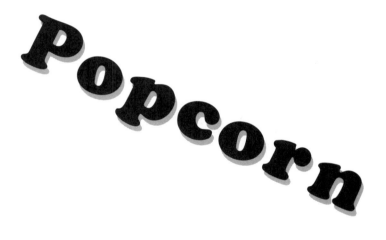

pretending to have the fingers act as if
they are popcorn kernels popping out
of the pan, use two hands with the
shape of ones but with index fingers
under the thumb and flick them off the
finger and move the hands up and
down several times

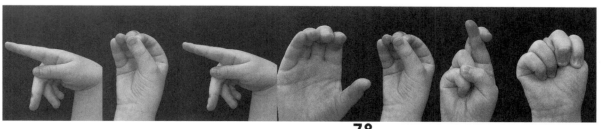

Potato

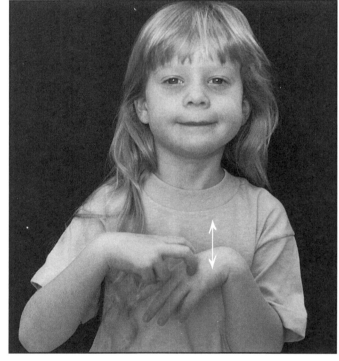

using a double x-shaped hand tap back of
other hand two times
(as if putting a fork in the potato)

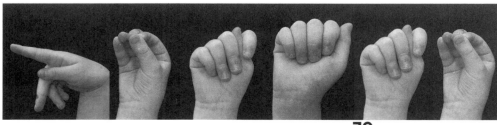

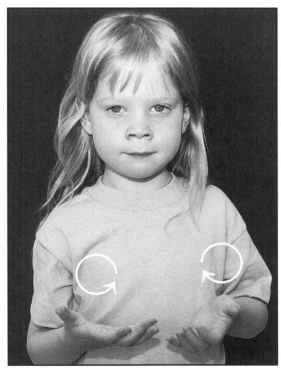

using slightly bend hands move up
and down in a
circular motion two times
(as if tossing a salad)

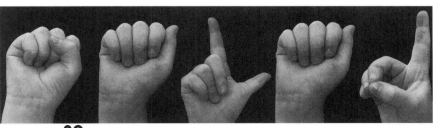

80

Sandwich

pretend to put food into sandwich
use hand palm up and put in other hand with
thumb on top of dominant hand, do this one
or two times

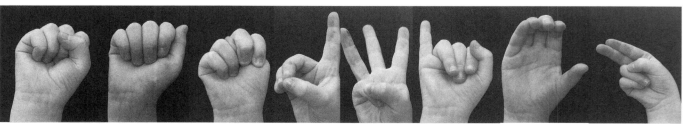

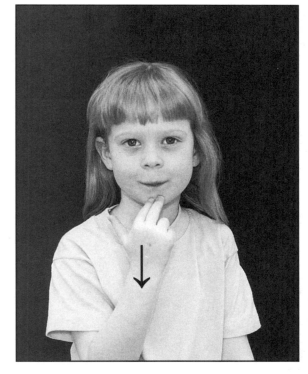

using a u-shaped hand and thumb out
move down
on chin two times
(same as sign for cute, also many other
variations for this sign)

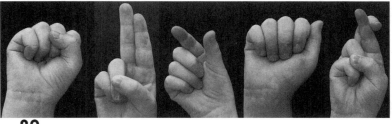

Vegetables

use the v-shaped hand put index finger on cheek and then put second finger on cheek (newer sign)

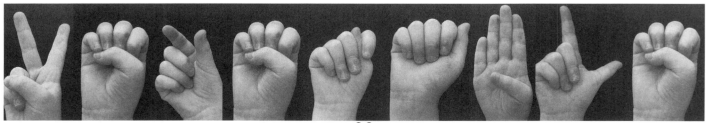

83

using a w-shaped hand place it on
the mouth (or chin) and bounce it off
the mouth two times outward
relates to drinking water

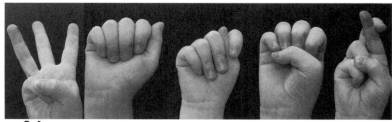

Colors

wiggle fingers in front of mouth

Red

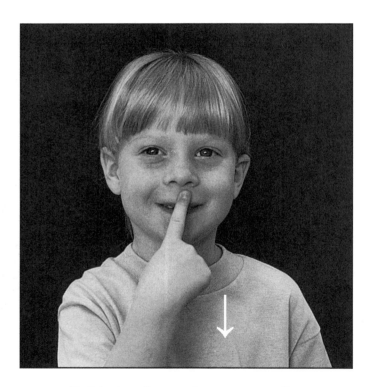

Pull index finger down across lips
and curl into an X shape

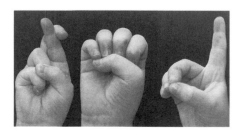

Pink

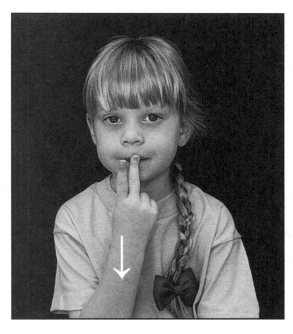

Use p-shaped hand and pull the
middle finger down across lips
two times

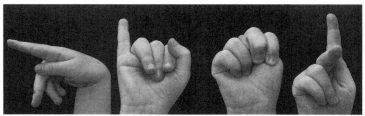

Orange

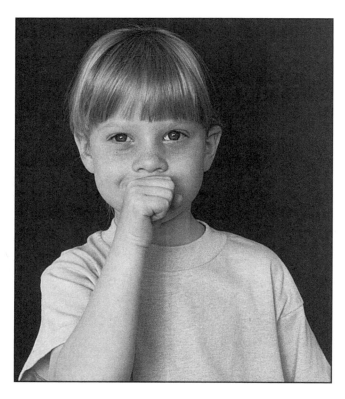

Use s-shaped hand opening and
closing the hand
(as if squeezing an orange)

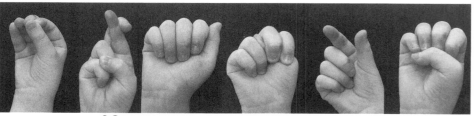

Yellow

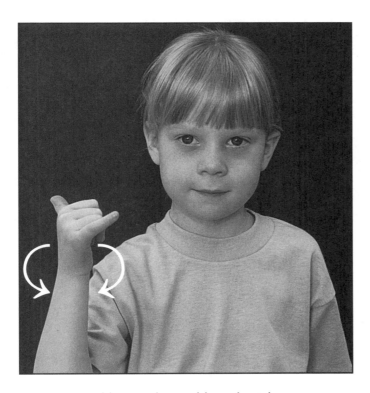

Use y-shaped hand and
twist the wrist back and forth

White

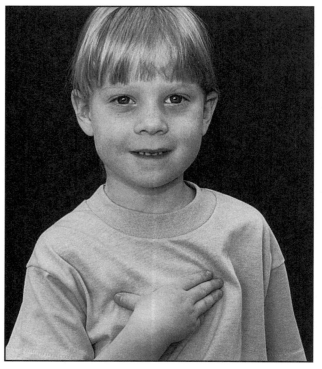

Use open-5 hand shape place on chest

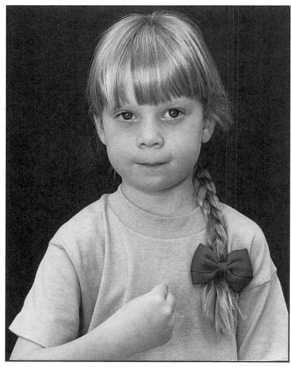

Move 5-hand out from chest and put fingers and thumb together to form a flat-o handshape

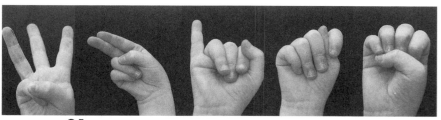

Black

Use index finger placed on forehead and
draw it back along the forehead

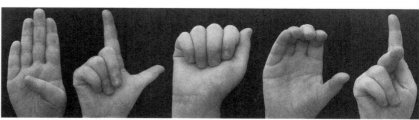

Green

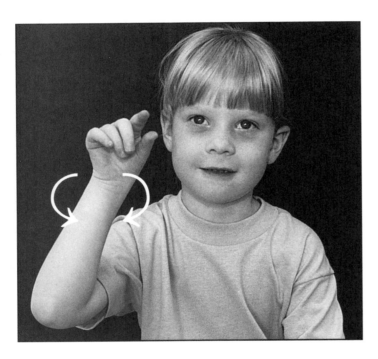

Use g-shaped hand twisting the wrist back and forth several times

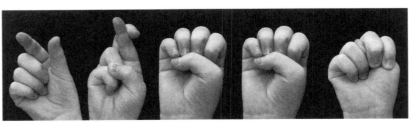

Blue

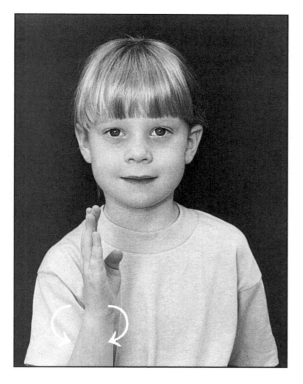

Use b-shaped hand twisting the
wrist back and forth several times

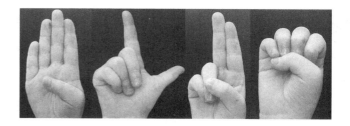

94

Purple

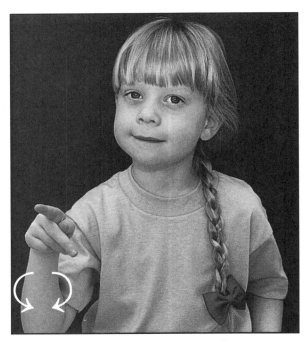

Use p-shaped hand twisting the wrist
back and forth several times

Brown

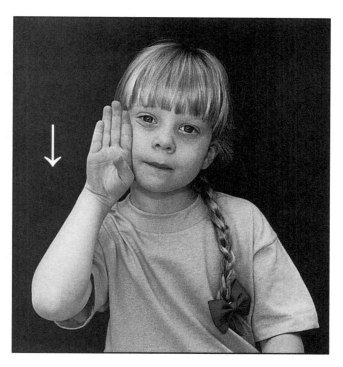

Use b-shaped hand, the index finger
placed on the cheek, the hand is drawn
straight down the cheek about one inch

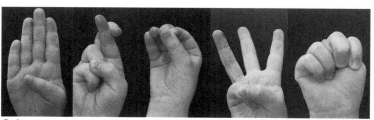

20

8

5

Numbers

4

1

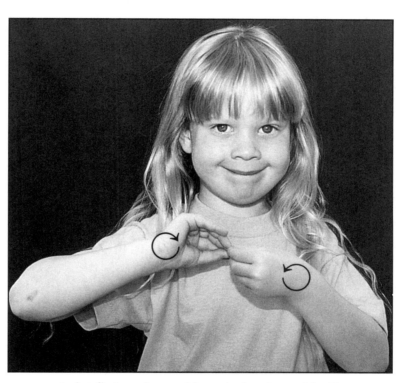

twist flat o-shaped hands back and forth
several times

7

17

3

12

2

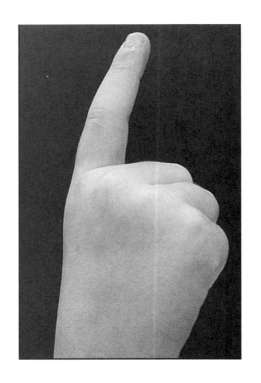

1

One

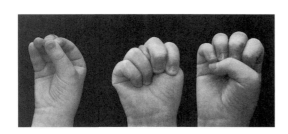

1 Hat

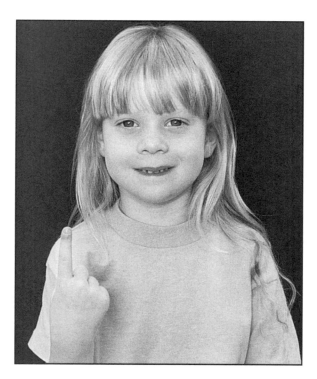

One

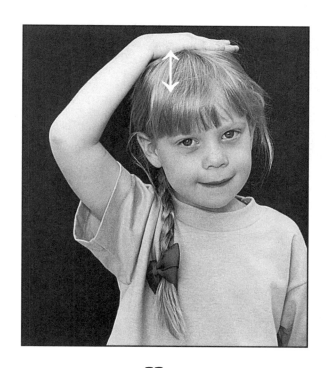

Hat

hand pats top of head two times

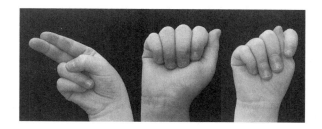

2

TWO

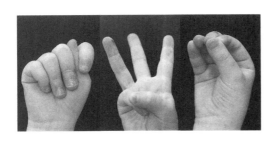

2 Horns

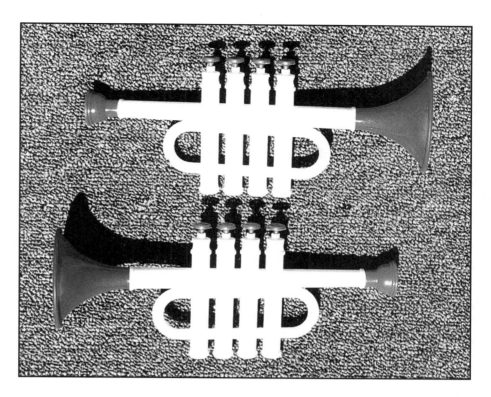

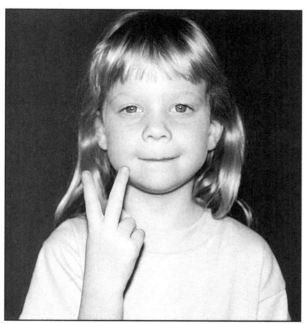

Two

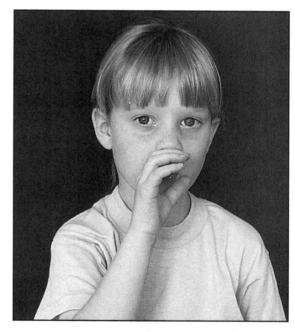

Horns

hand at mouth - pretend to blow the horn and push the valves

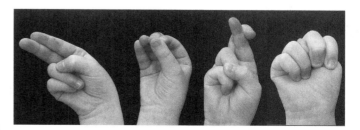

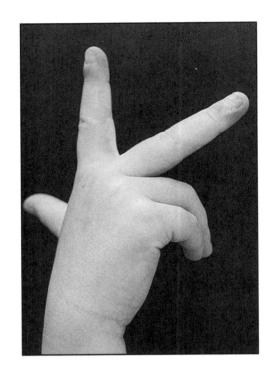

3

Three

3 Boats

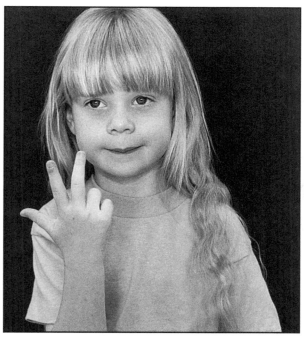

Three

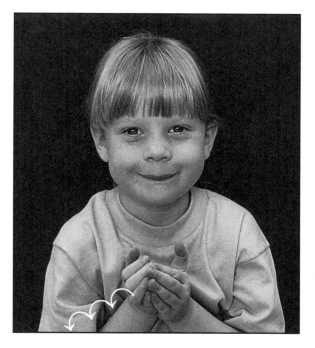

Boats

Make the shape of a boat with your two hands and move the hands forward as if boat is moving forward

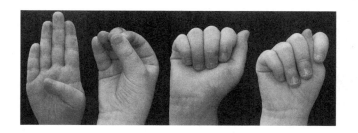

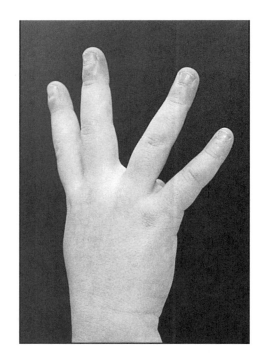

4

Four

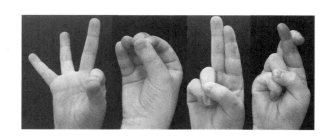

4
Buckets

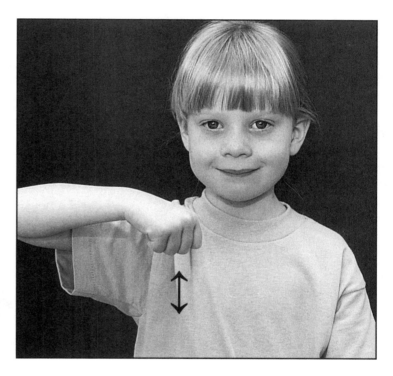

Four

Buckets

use s-shaped hand grasping the handle of a
bucket, bounce once or twice for emphasis

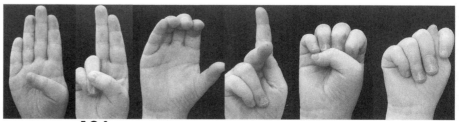

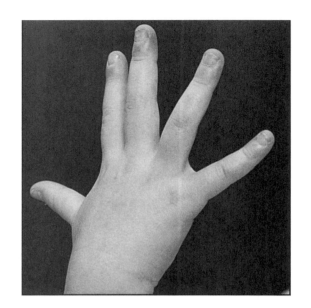

5

Five

5 Paint Trays

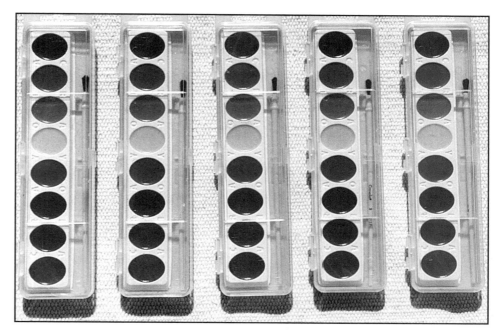

Five

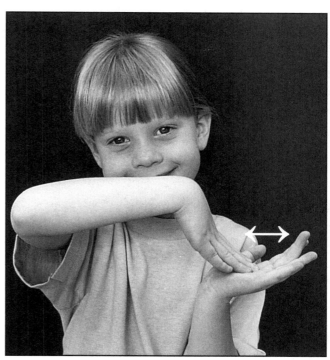

Paints

using your hand as a paint brush going
back and forth one time

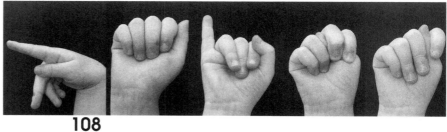

108

● ● ● ● ● ●

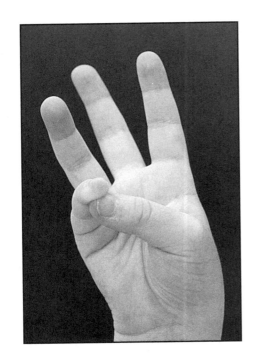

6

Six

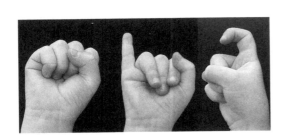

6 Toothbrushes

Six

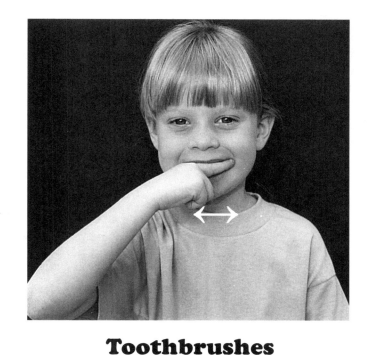

Toothbrushes

using your index finger, pretend you are
brushing your teeth two times

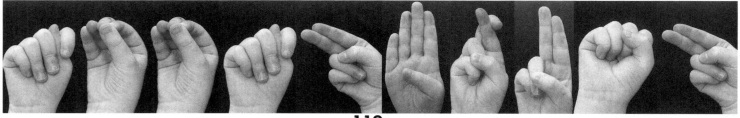

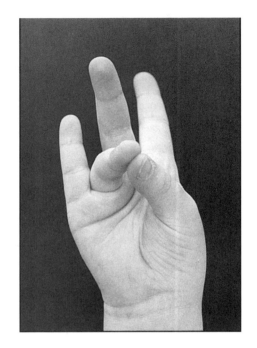

7

Seven

7 people

Seven

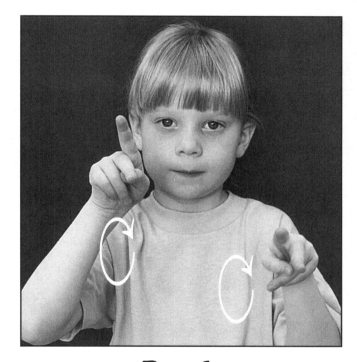

People

use p-shaped hands in a circular motion
like peddling a bike

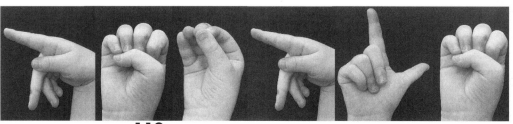

8

Eight

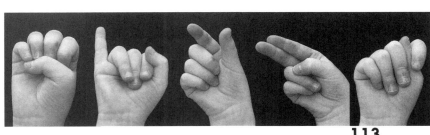

8 spoons

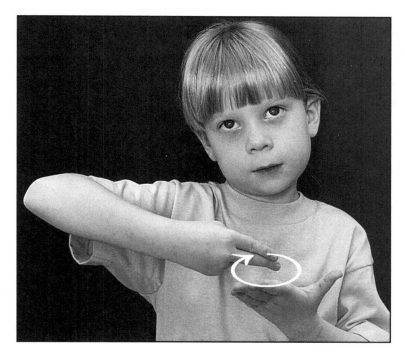

Eight

Spoons

using u-shaped hand representing the spoon,
move spoon in scooping motion to the other hand
which represents a dish or bowl

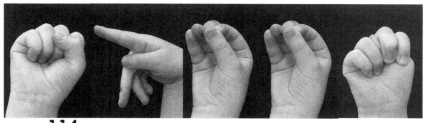

114

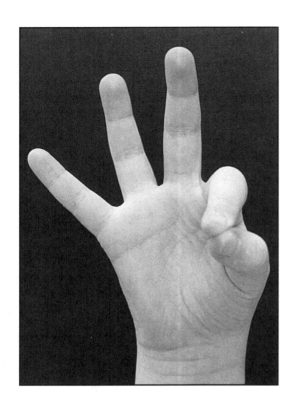

9

Nine

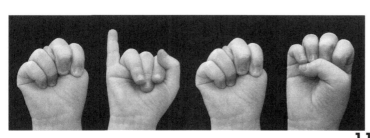

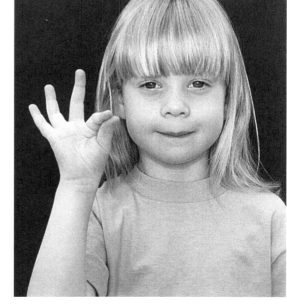

9 Balloons

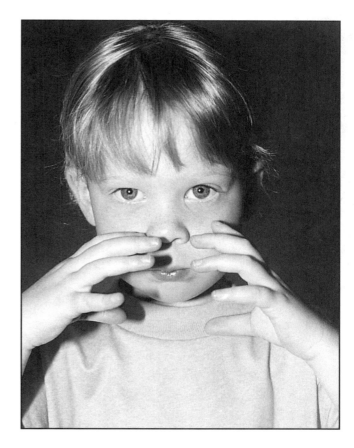

Balloons

hold s-shaped hand to mouth and opening hands as if blowing up a balloon

10

Ten

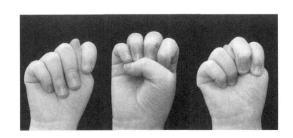

117

10 Keys

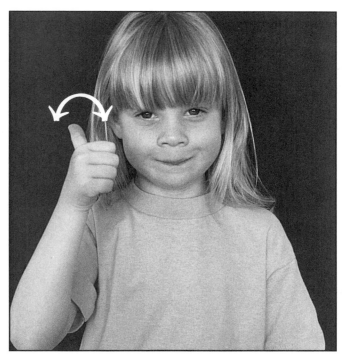

Ten

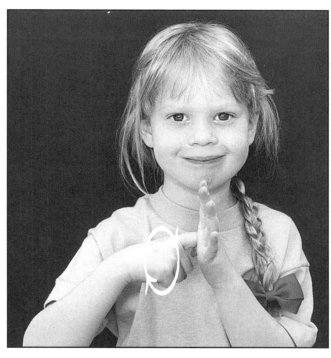

Keys

use x-shaped hand, turn as if turning a key
back and forth several times

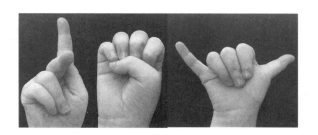

118

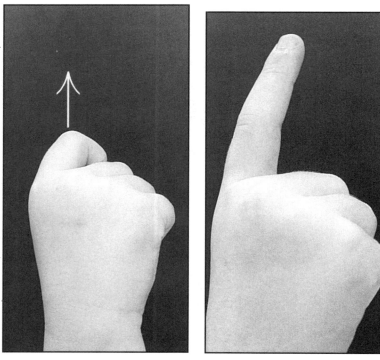

Flick index finger off of thumb to form a one

11

Eleven

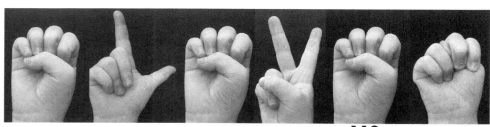

11 balls

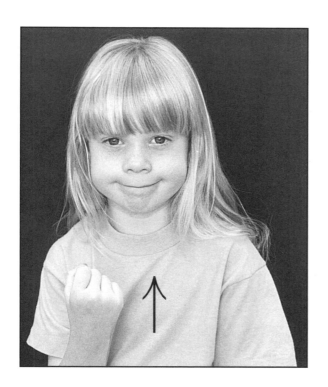

Eleven

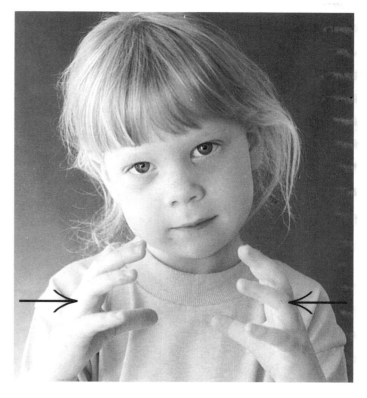

Balls

open curved fingers, palms facing toward
each other with tips of fingers touching to
make a shape of the ball

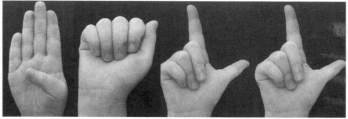

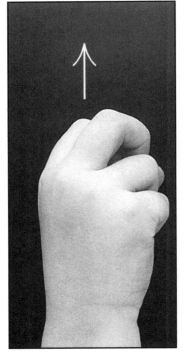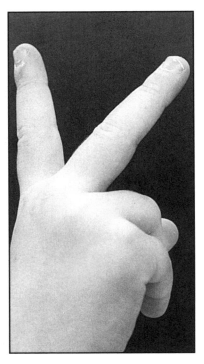

12

flick index and middle fingers off of thumb to show
the two fingers

Twelve

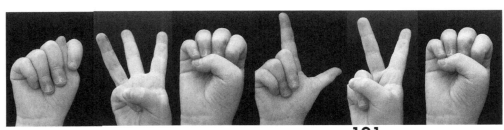

12
flowers

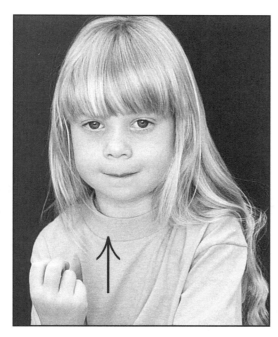

Twelve

Flowers

place finger tips on right side of
nose and arc to left side of nose
to pretend smelling a flower

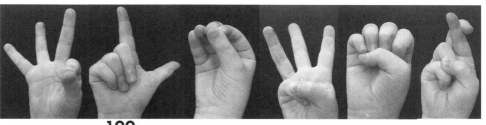

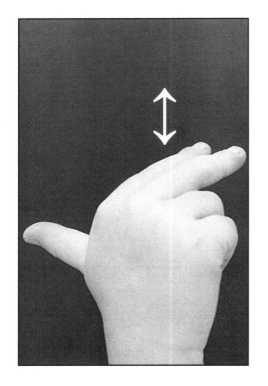

move index and middle finger
together back and forth slightly
with thumb sticking out
not moving

13

Thirteen

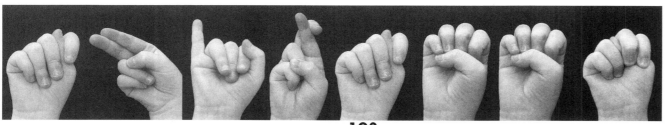

13
dresses

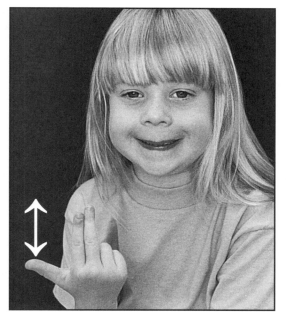

Thirteen

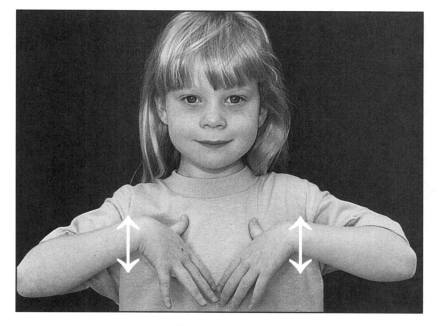

Dresses

move 5-shaped hands downward with thumbs on chest
(as if putting on a dress)

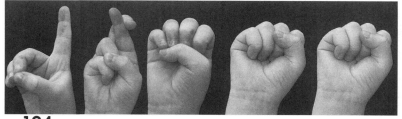

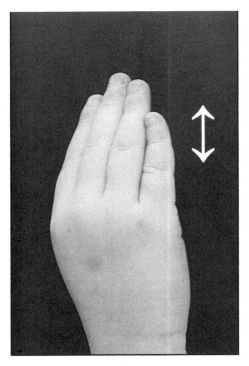

close four fingers together over
thumb several times

14

Fourteen

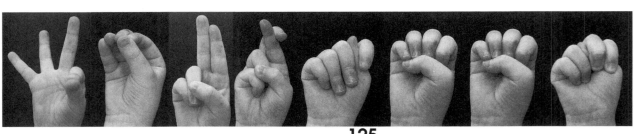

14
candies

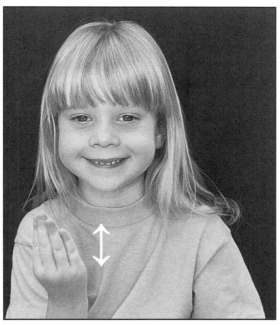

Fourteen

Candies

place index finger on the side of the face and
twist two times

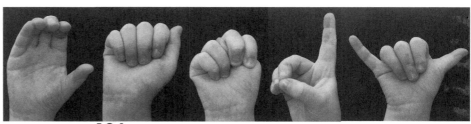

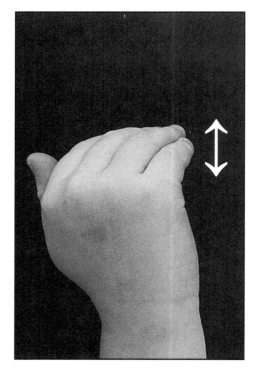

same as fourteen but with
thumb out

15

Fifteen

15 cars

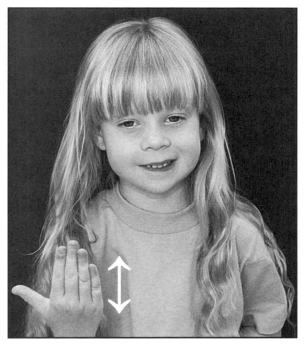

Fifteen

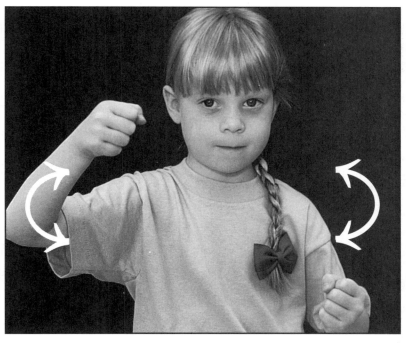

Cars

pretend holding a steering wheel and move
slightly to left and right as if driving

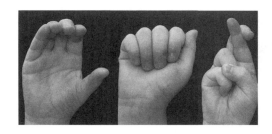

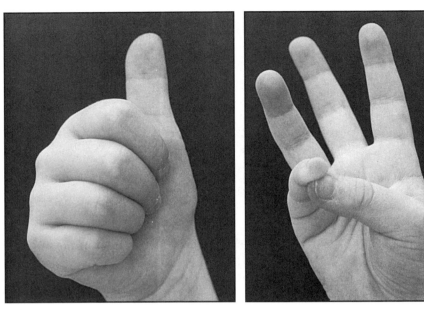

sign ten then six in one movement outward

16

Sixteen

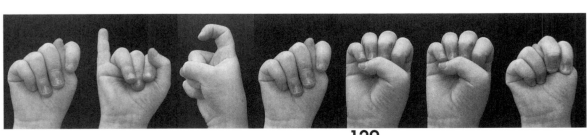

16
Buttons

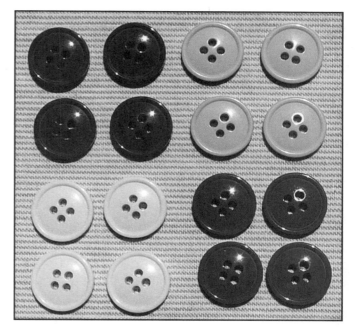

Sixteen

Buttons

f-shape with thumb down on chest to show a button and tap three buttons moving downward on shirt

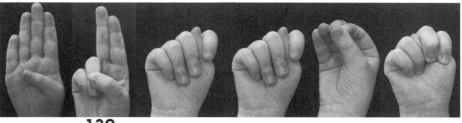

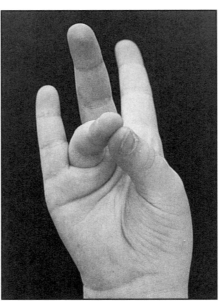

sign ten then six in one movement outward

17

Seventeen

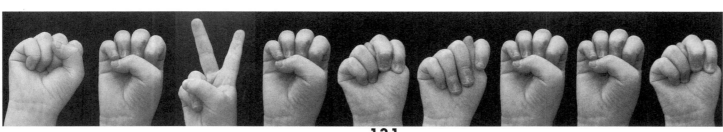

17 blocks

Seventeen

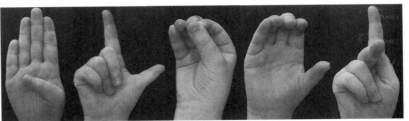

Blocks

flat hand-shape with palms inward
towards each other marking the two
sides of a block then move them to
do top and bottom

sign ten then eight in one movement outward

18

Eighteen

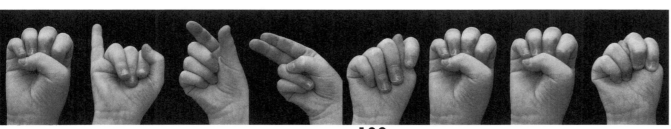

18 eggs

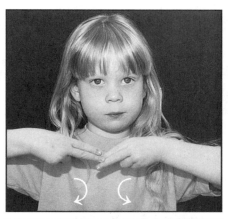

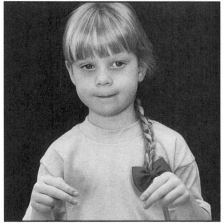

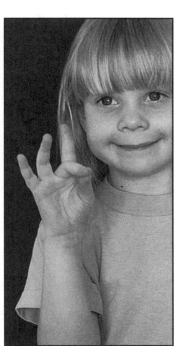

Eighteen

Eggs

pretend cracking open an egg
move two u-shaped hands out
from each other once or twice

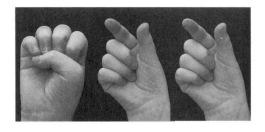

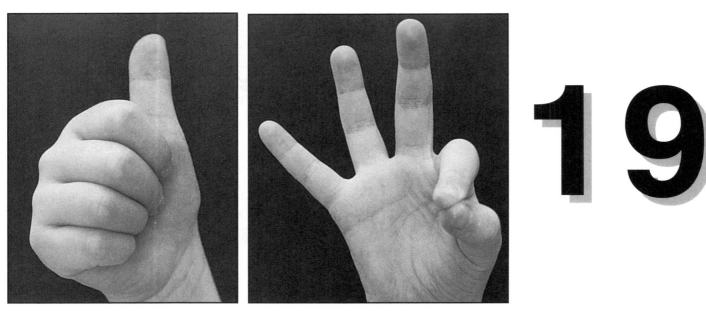

sign ten then nine in one movement outward

19

Nineteen

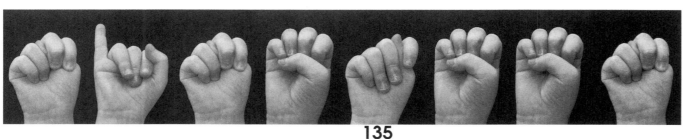

19 marbles

Nineteen

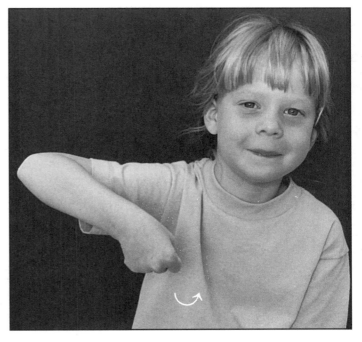

Marbles

pretend shooting marbles
flick thumb off of x-shaped hand

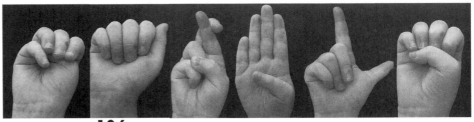

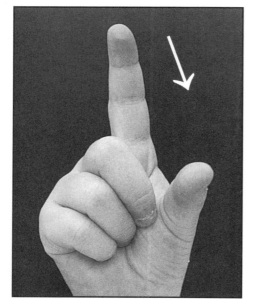

tap index finger down to
thumb two times

20

Twenty

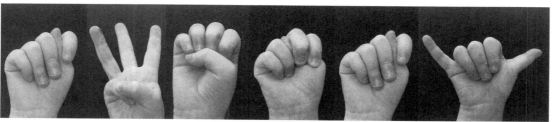

20

markers

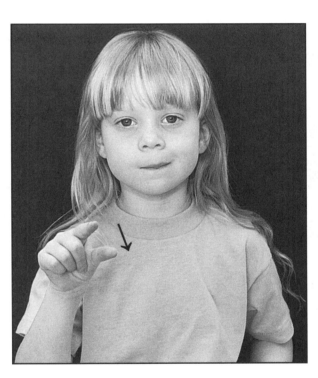

Twenty

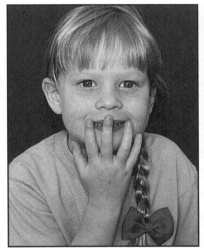 

Marker (color + writer)

open five-shaped
hand with palm in
wiggle fingers over
chin several times

thumb and index finger
together as if were hold-
ing a pen or marker and
slide across palm as if
writing

138

Opposites

Stop

On
Off

Big
Small

In
Out

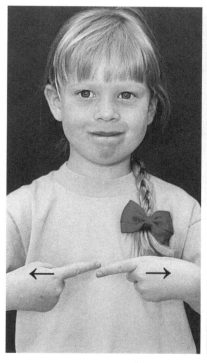 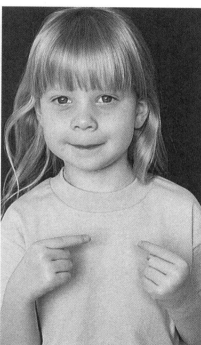

Opposite

Use both index fingers touching each
other then pull them apart to about six
inches away from each other

 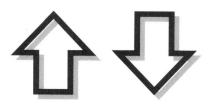 

Big

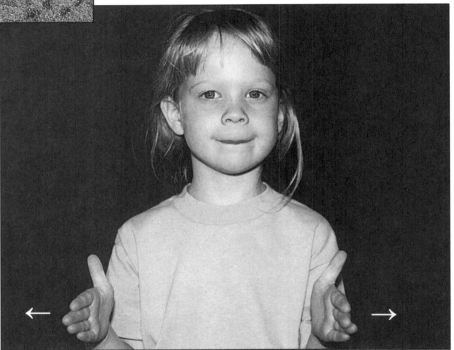

with both hands palms towards each other and about 2 or 3 inches apart move them away from each other till they are about a foot apart
as showing how big something is

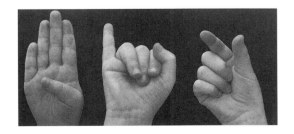

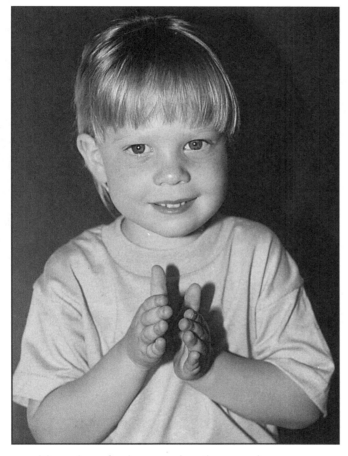

Small

with palms facing each other and
about 4 or 5 inches apart move them
towards each other (about an 2 inches apart) two times
as if showing how small
something is

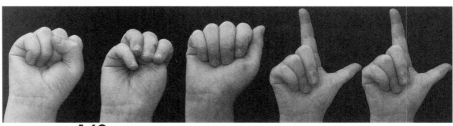

142

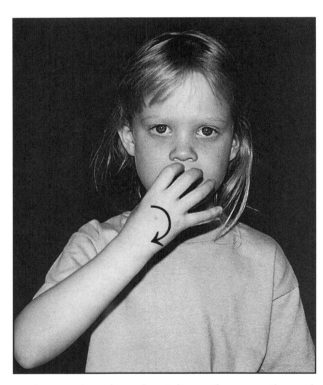

using a claw hand put it on the mouth and then quickly move it away and to the right as if the mouth was hot

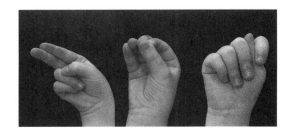

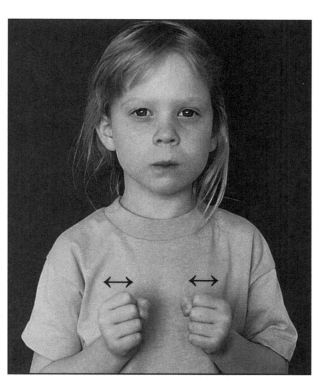

use both hands near the chest in an s-shaped hand then move them back and forth towards each other
as if being cold and shivering

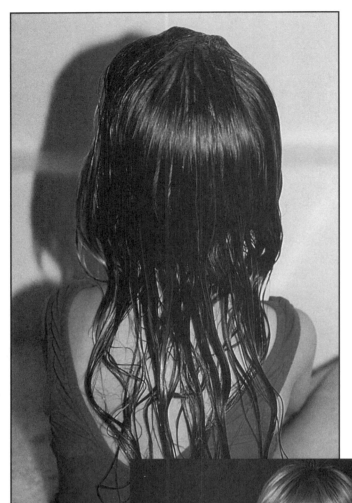

Wet

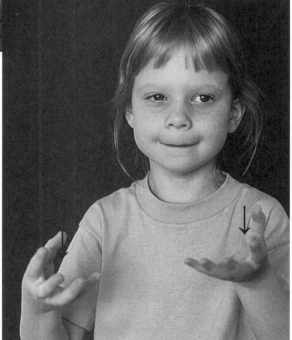

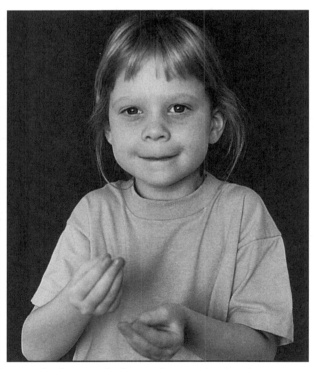

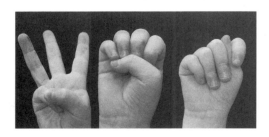

with both hands out in front of chest then take both open
hands with thumbs up and move thumb and four fingers
towards each other and ends in a flat-o shape
(as if holding a wet object in your hands and feeling it)

145

Dry

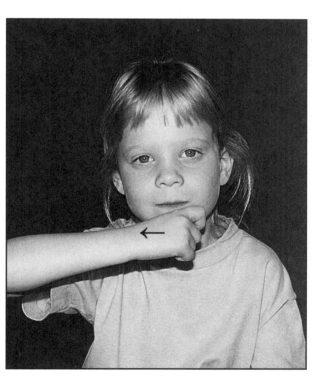

use the x-shaped hand and put it on the
left side of the chin then pull it across the
chin to the other side
as if wiping off chin or lips

Happy

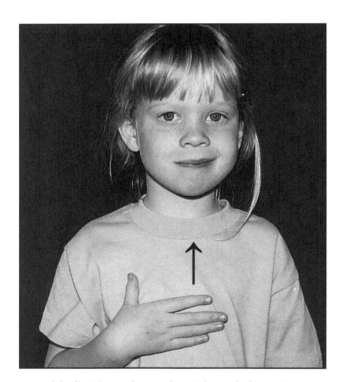

with flat hand on chest brush it up two
times moving up and off the chest

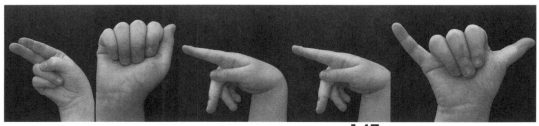

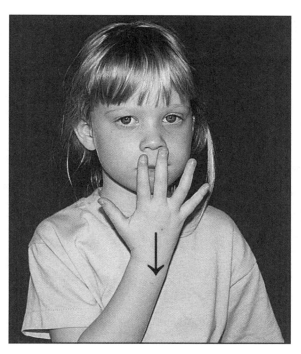

use an open five-hand in front of face
and pull it down slowly several inches
as if showing sadness

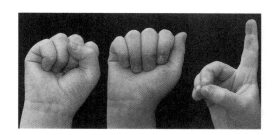

Clean

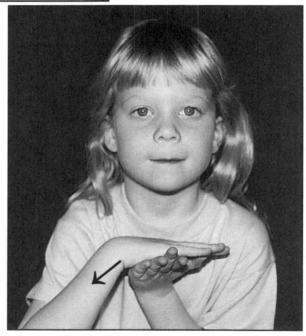

use two flat hands with one on top of the
other at right angles (perpendicular)
then move the top hand
across the other
as if wiping the dirt away

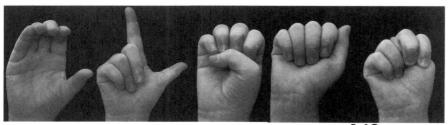

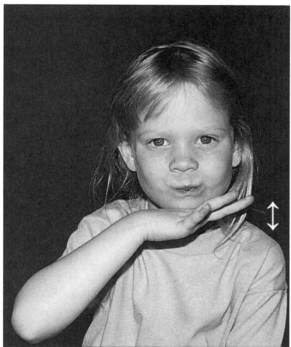

hold hand under chin with fingers
pointing to the left then wiggle the
fingers up and down several times

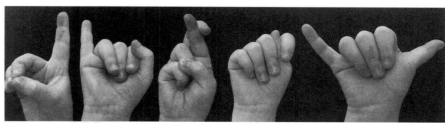

150

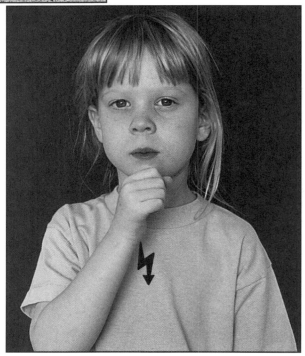

using the s-shaped hand put it on the chin and move it down in a zig-zag motion
as if pulling on a long beard

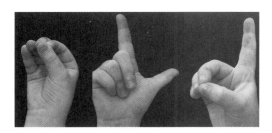

151

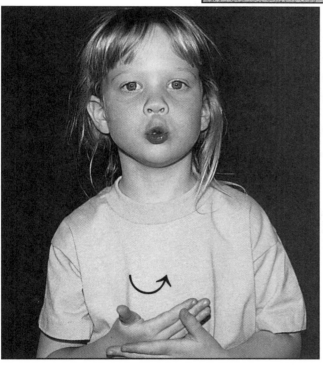

with one hand in front of the body (non-dominant hand) take the dominant hand and brush it across the other hand once

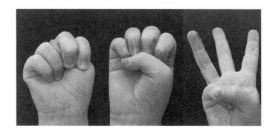

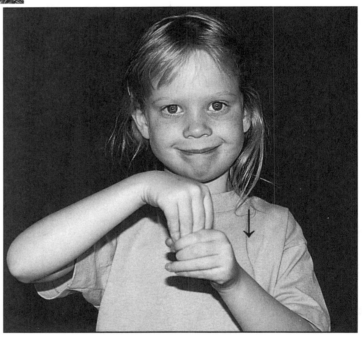

In

use the non-dominant hand and make an o-
shaped hand then take the other hand, shaped
as a flat-o and put it into the other hand
as if placing an object in the other

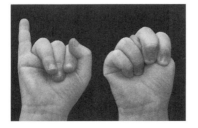

153

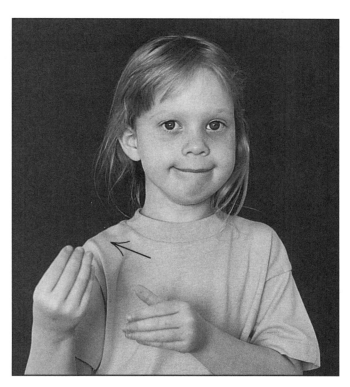

similar to in but in the opposite direction
use the in sign and move the hand out of the
o-shaped hand
as if taking it out of the other hand

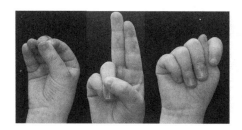

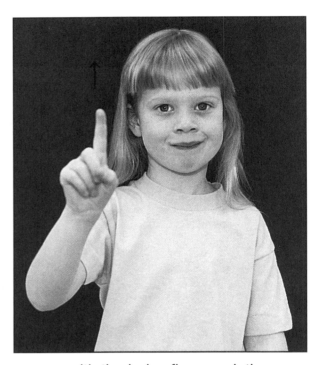

with the index finger pointing up
move it up a little once
as if pointing up

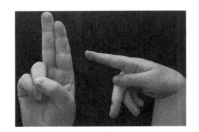

155

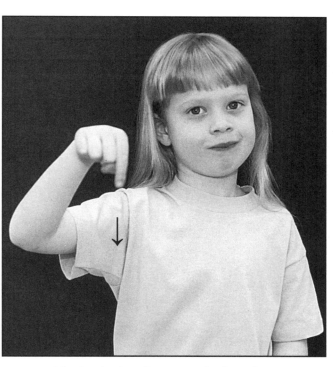

with the index finger pointing down
move it down a little once
as if pointing down

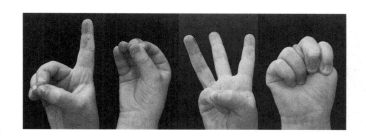

Open

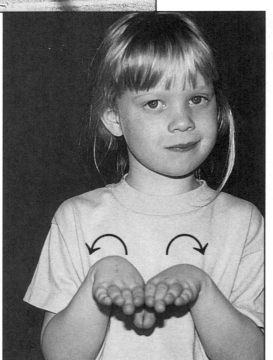

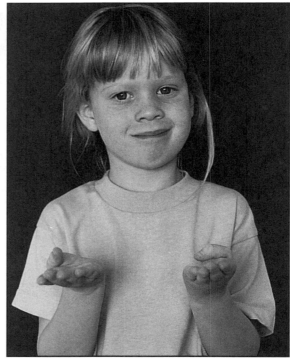

take the two flat b-shaped hands side
by side with palms facing downward
turn both hands so that both palms are
facing up
as if opening a box

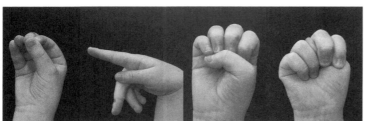

157

Close

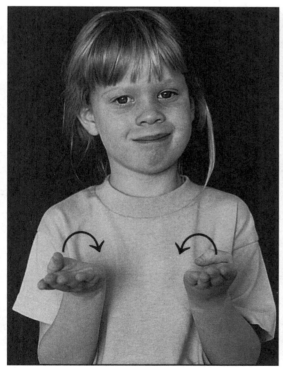

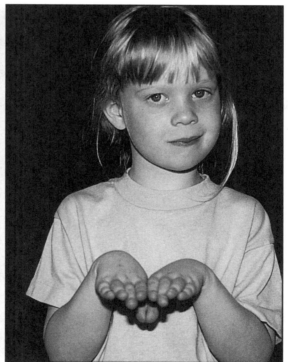

similar to open but the opposite
take the two flat b-shaped hands side-
by-side and with palms facing upward
turn both hands so that the palms are
facing down
as if closing a box

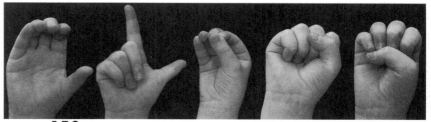

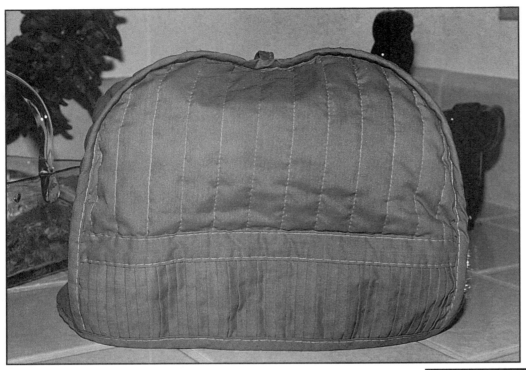

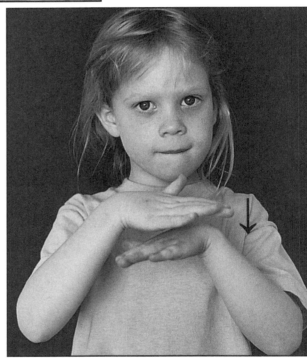

place both hands with palms facing downward in front of body then put the dominant hand on top of the other hand
as if putting something on it

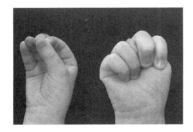

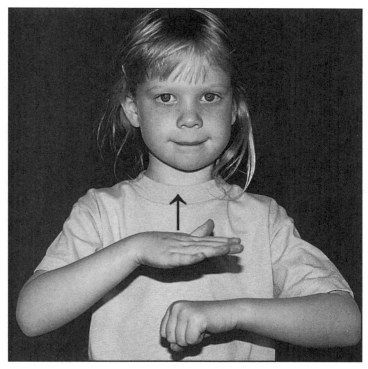

similar to on but the opposite
place both hands with palms facing downward in
front of body then take the dominant hand off the
top of the other hand
as if taking something off of it

Short

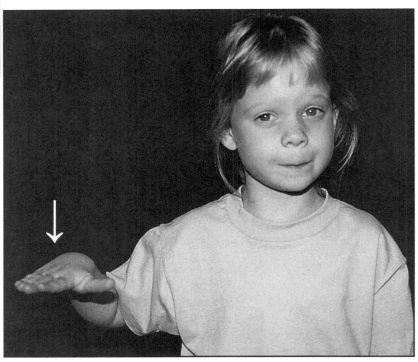

put the hand to the side of the body and indicate that something is short with the palm facing down

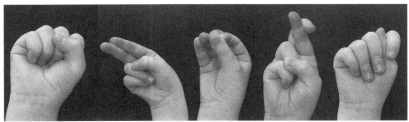

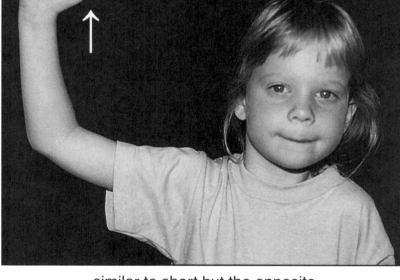

similar to short but the opposite
put the hand to the side of the body and indicate that
something is tall with the palm facing down

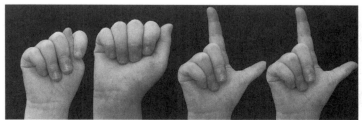

162

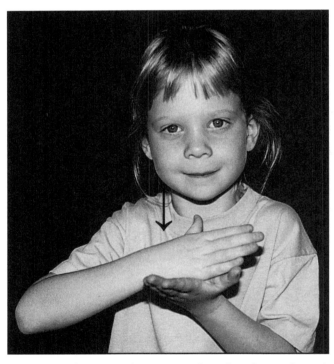

use two flat hands, move the dominant hand
on above the other with the side of the hand
touching the other
as if to indicate a cutting short

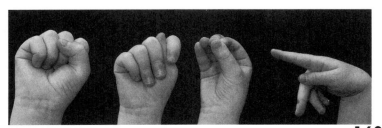

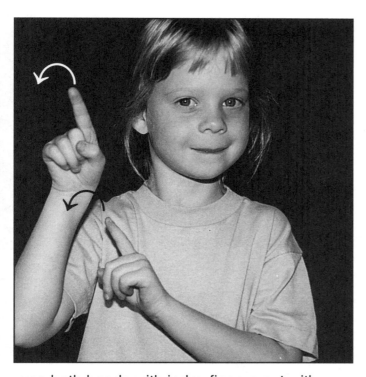

use both hands with index fingers out with one
hand below the other move them outwards
as if indicating going towards a place

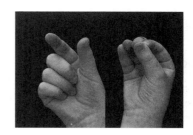

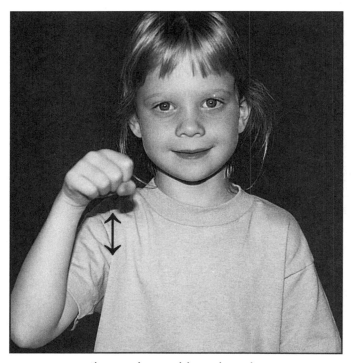

use the s-shaped hand and move
it up and down
as if the hand was a head nodding yes

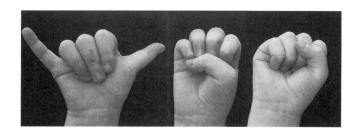

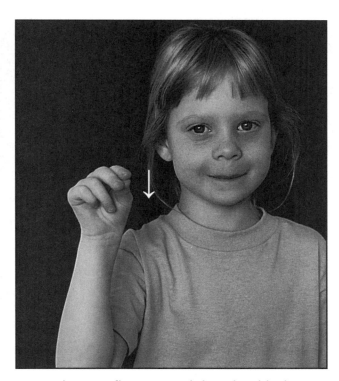

use the two fingers and thumb with them
separated move the fingers
and thumb to touch
as if snapping a no with a duck beak

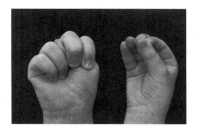

Good

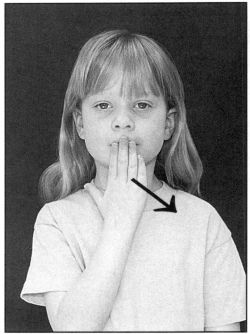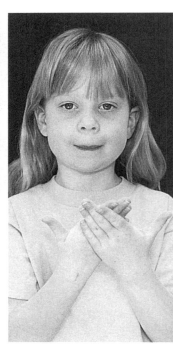

move the one flat hand out from the mouth towards the
other hand so that the back of the right hand touches the
palm of other other hand

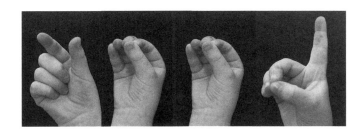

Bad

use the 5-shaped hand palm inward on the mouth
and move in a downward arcing twist

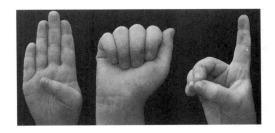

Animals

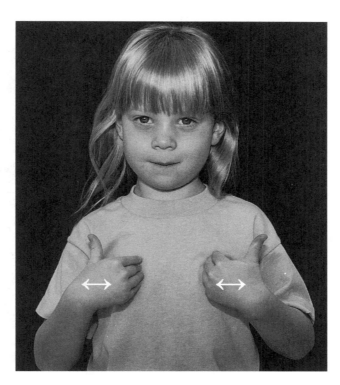

curved fingertips on chest anchored
arms move towards each other
several times

Bear

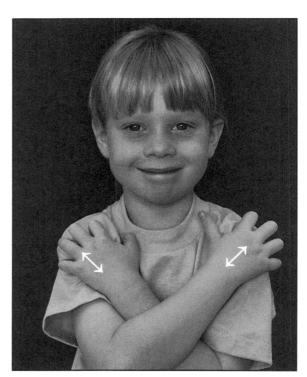

cross wrists of clawed hands and
scratch upper chest

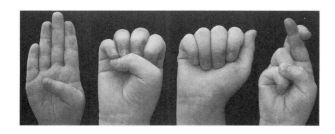

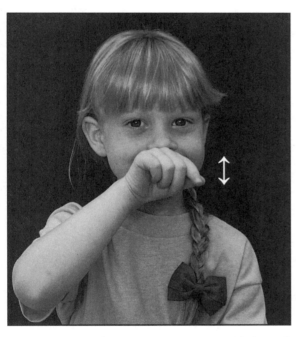

place back of hand on mouth with hand in shape of (number 20 or) bird beak, open the beak several times

Cat

moving your hands back towards cheeks
using an f-shaped hand backwards across
cheeks one or more times
(as if to feel the whiskers of a cat)

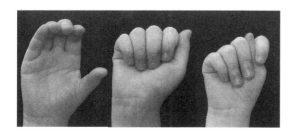

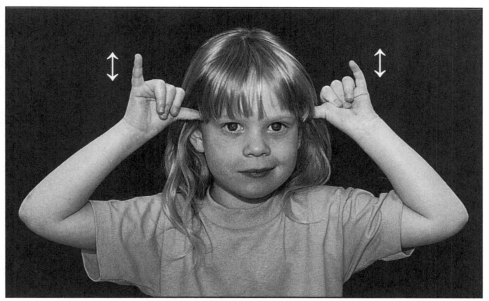

Cow

pretend to imitate the horns of a cow
using y-shaped hand place thumbs on sides of head anchored
turn hands up and down two times

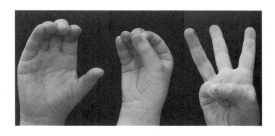

Dog

pat side of leg with hand
several times
variation: also do snap of
fingers on dominant hand to
indicate calling a dog

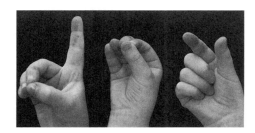

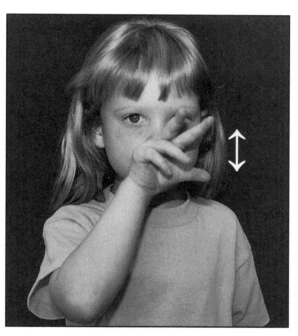

Duck

pretend to make the shape and action
of a duck beak
put back of hand on mouth
using thumb on bottom and first two fingers on top, move up and down
as if quacking

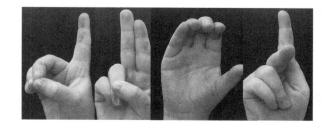

176

Elephant

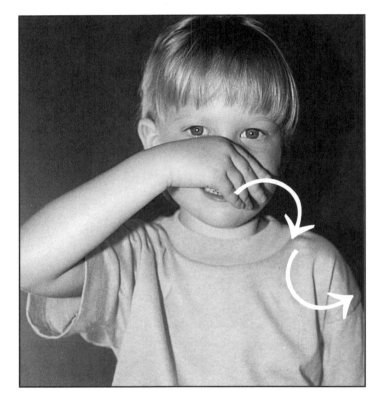

flat or b-shaped hand moves down and out
(as if showing an elephant trunk)

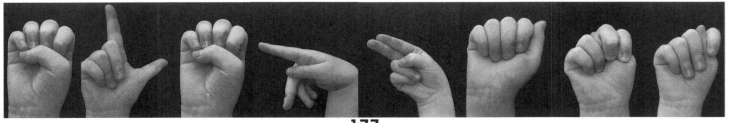

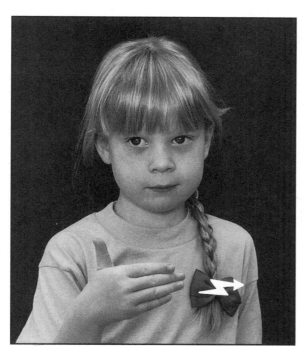

with flat hand thumb up flutter hand like
a fish swimming in the water
move hand outward several inches

Fish

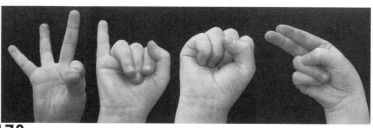

Giraffe

pretend making the long neck
of a giraffle
use c-shaped hand and move up and
outward

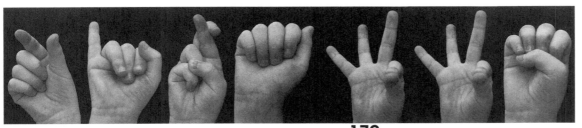

Goat

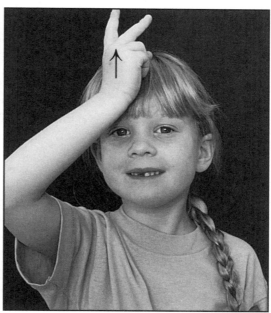

pretend making the goatee and horns of a goat
with 12-shaped hand flick off of chin with thumb on chin and
off of head once each

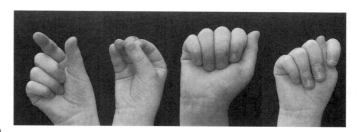

Horse

pretend to make the horse ear moving
use h-shape with thumb out
place on thumb on temple anchored and
move fingers up and down two times

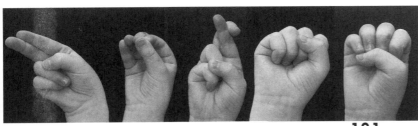

181

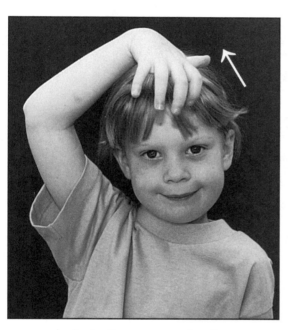

imitate the mane of a lion
with claw hand on forehead
move hand back through hair

Lion

182

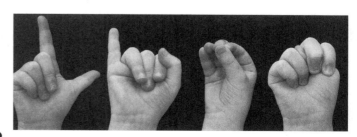

Monkey

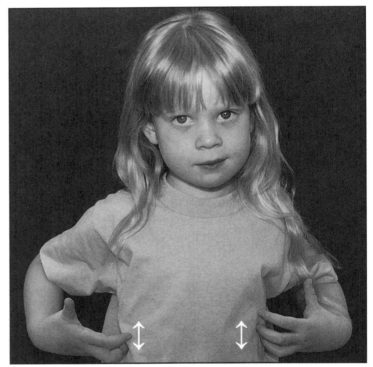

pretend to scractch sides like a monkey
use claw-shaped hand up sides of body
two times

183

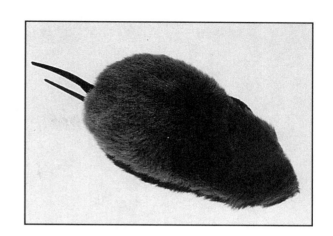

refs to the small wriggling nose
of a mouse
put index finger on nose and brush
past two times

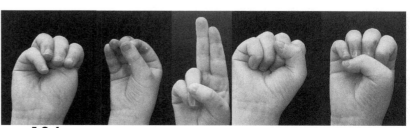

Pig

refers to dirty
put hand under chin with fingers together
move fingers together up and down two times

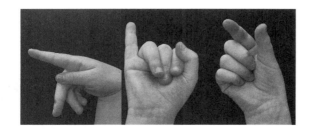

pretend making moving ears
of a rabbit
put hands facing backwards on sides
of head with h-shaped hand
with thumb out (similar to horse)
and move fingers up and
down two times

Rabbit

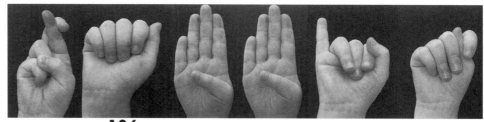

Sheep

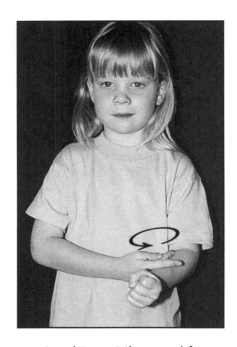

pretend to cut the wool from
a sheep
with v-shaped hand
(imaginary scissors)
run back up arm in a circle
several times

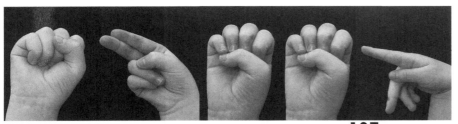

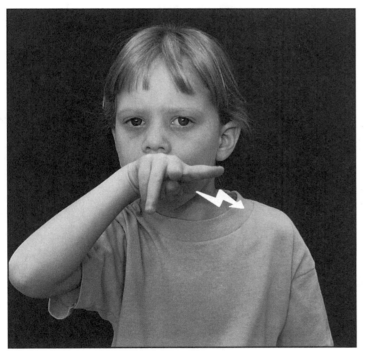

Snake

pretend to use hand as tongue of snake moving
use v-shaped hand (or two) with back of hand
on chin move hand forward in a zig-zag motion

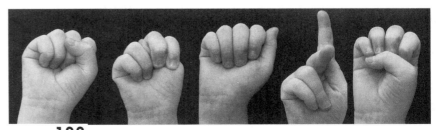

Zebra

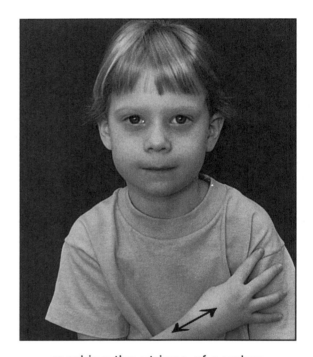

marking the stripes of a zebra
with a four-shaped hand
place on opposite forearm (not shoulder as shown) and draw stripes
across arm several times

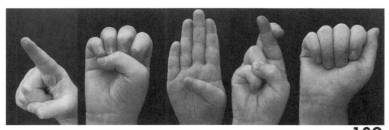

More Signs

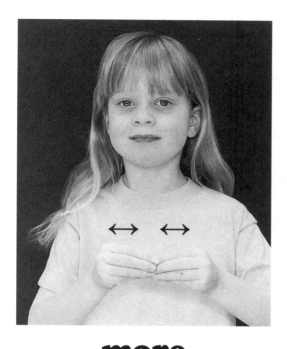

more

With flat-o shaped hands touch the tips of the fingers together then pull them several times

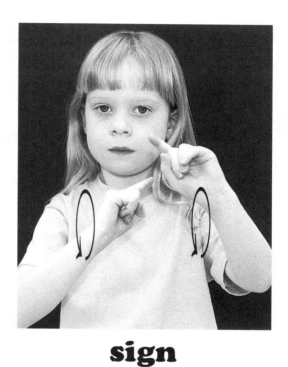

sign

On both hands have the index finger out and move them in circular motions several times as if riding a bike with one hand at the top of the circle and the other at the bottom

like, love

please, sorry, thank you

who, what, where, when, why

boy, girl, mom, dad

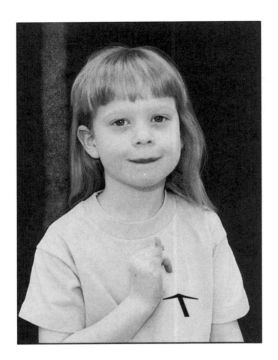

I

I-shaped hand place thumb part on chest once (similar to me)

you

With the index finger point to the person

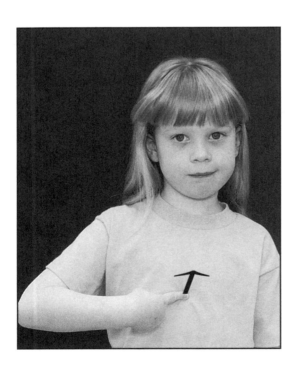

me

With the index finger point to yourself by placing the tip of the index finger on your chest or near your chest

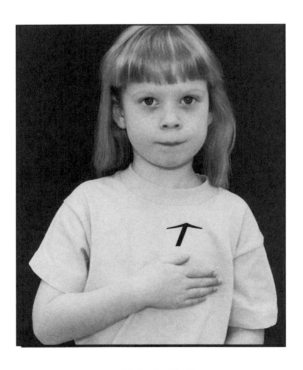

my

With the flat hand place the palm on the chest or near your chest

we

With the w-shaped hand swing the hand from right shoulder to left shoulder as if indicating a group of people

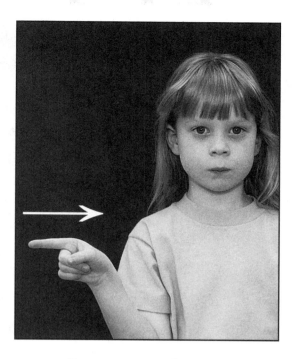

they / you (plural)

With the index finger point to the group of people or objects in a sweeping motion (in one direction or the other)

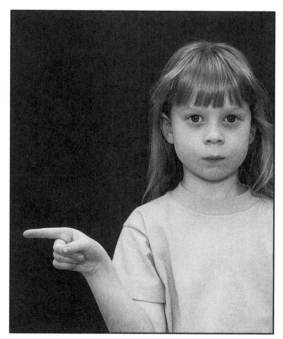

he/she/it

Point with index finger to the person or object (same as you)

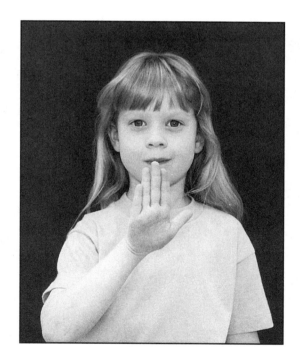

your

With flat hand and palm out push palm toward person once

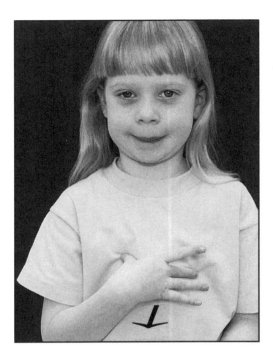

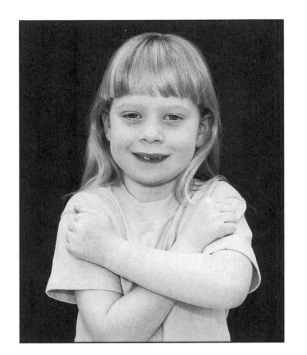

I
love
you

like

With thumb and middle finger apart place on chest and pull thumb and middle finger together until they touch and pull out from chest once

love

Using to closed fists (or s-shaped hands) put them on the chest as if hugging someone

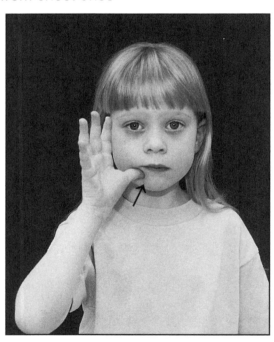

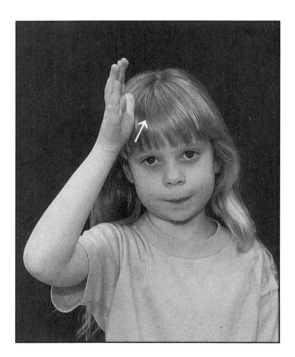

mom

With 5-shaped hand tap thumb on chin twice

dad

With 5-shaped hand tap thumb on forehead twice

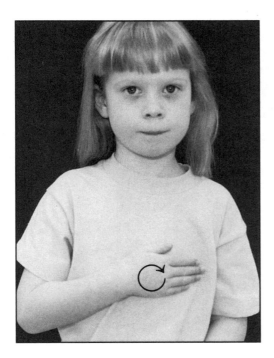

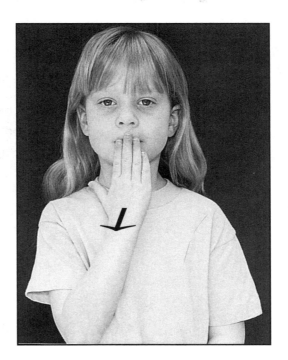

please

use the flat hand with palm on the chest and circle make a clock-wise circle once or twice

thank you

use the flat hand with palm facing mouth with tips of fingers on lips and move outward once with a small nod of the head (as if throwing a kiss) also used for "you are welcome"

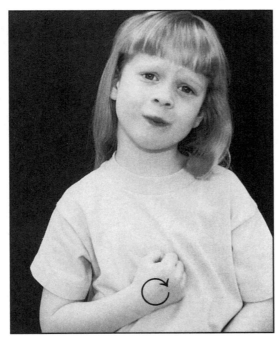

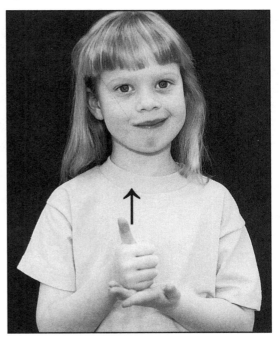

sorry

use s-shaped hand with thumb on chest and make a clockwise circle on chest once or twice (similar to please)

help

place the ten-shaped hand on top of the non-dominant hand with palm up and raise both upward six inches once (as if the left hand was helping the right hand move up)

hello

use b-shaped and place on forehead and move outward (as if
saluting)

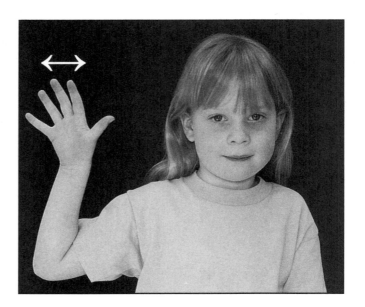

goodbye

wave goodbye (as you normally wave goodbye to your friends)

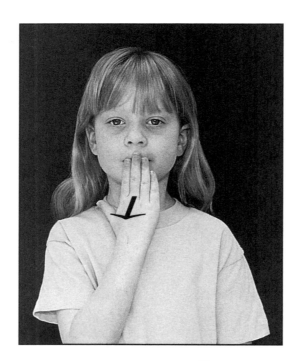

good

(similar to thank you) but with hand
touching other hand - other hand is
wasit high 12 inches out from waist

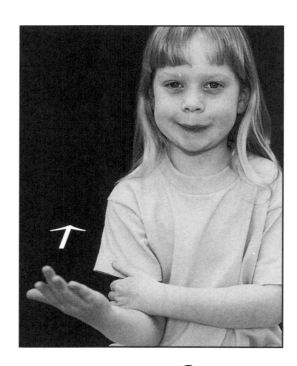

morning

place left hand on crease in arm at
elbow plam down - with right arm -
flat hand palm up - move upwards
once (as if the sun was coming up
from the horizon)

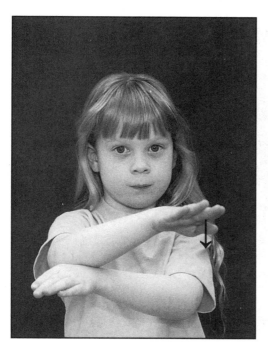

afternoon

left arm under the elbow of the right arm palm down move the right arm downward with palm down (as if the sun was going down)

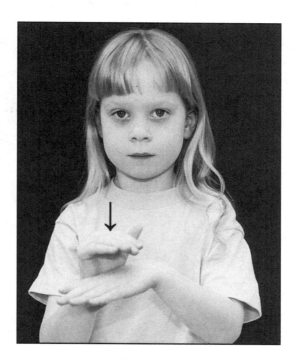

night

with left arm out and the hand in a fist or s-shape place right hand on top of left hand using the bent-hand shape (as if the sun is going down)

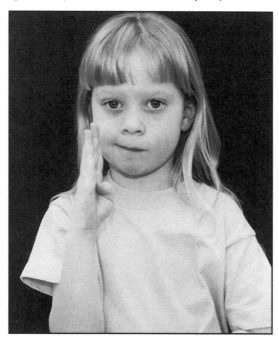

noon

with left arm out palm down place elbow of right arm on top of the other hand with b-shaped hand and palm to left (as if the sun was straight up above) **198**

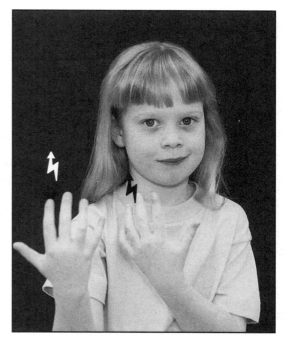

wait

with both hands and palms up wiggle fingers up and down several times

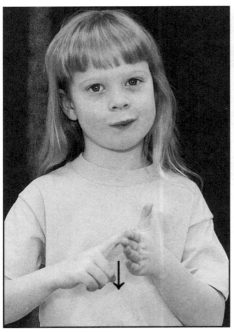
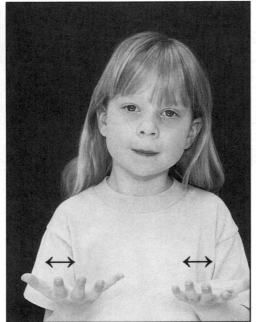

what

with left hand out palm facing right use the index finger on the right hand and brush it downwards against the fingers of the other hand

variation two: with 5-shaped hands palm up move both sideways several times

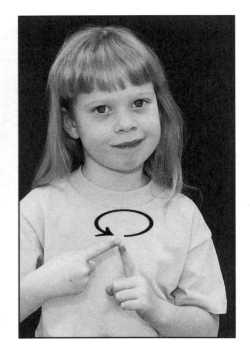

when

with the index finger of the left hand out make a circle clockwise with the right index finger touch the tip of the left hand with starting and ending the circle (as if drawing the circle of a clock)

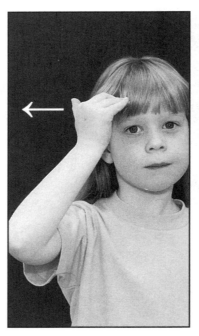
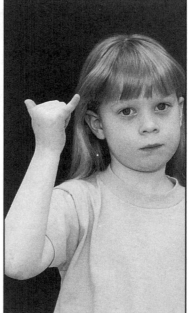

where

with the index finger wave it left and right several times

why

with the flat hand palm down and tips of fingers on the forehead, move outward into a y-shaped hand

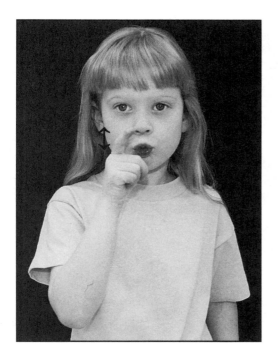

who

(there are two ways to sign who)
with the L-shaped hand touching
the chin wiggle the index finger
several times

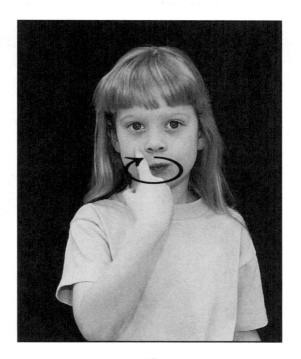

who

with the index finger near the mouth draw a
counter-clockwise circle around the mouth
(have mouth shaped like you are saying who)

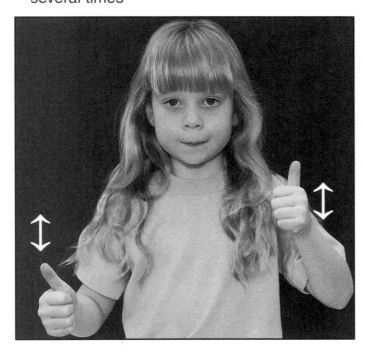

which

using both hands in the ten-shape, move the
hands up and down - one up while the other
goes down

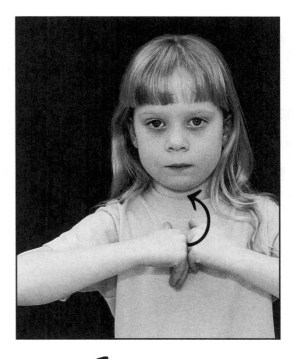

how

with both hands in bent hand shapes
and back of hands touching and
palms down slowly turn the hands
towards the chest and then up once

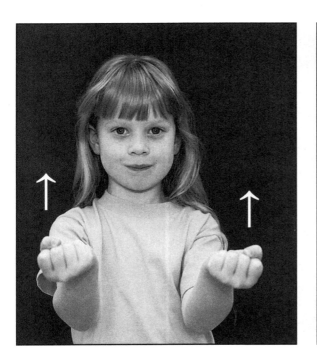 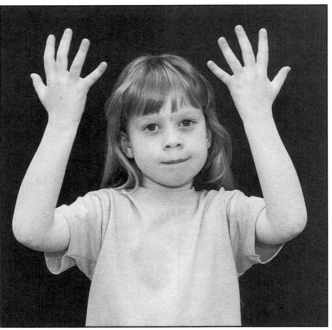

how much
how many

depends on context, but usually the price or cost sign is added after how much
with closed hands and out in front of the body palms up move both hands upwards and
open hands till they are equal with the head (as if throwing money into the air)

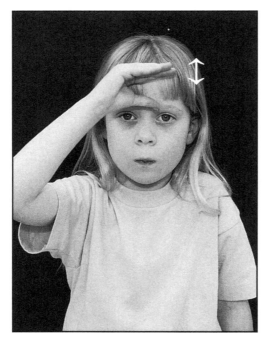 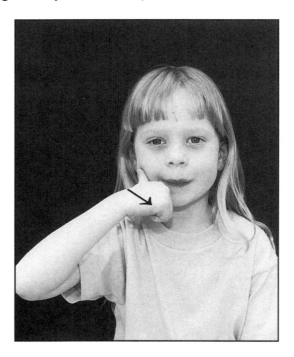

boy

with hand near forehead with flat
hand and thumb out (down) bring
thumb and fingers together twice
(as if touch the brim of a ball cap)

girl

with the ten-shaped hand and thumb
touching the face on right cheek
move thumb down along the jaw line
to chin (as if drawing the line of a
bonnett string)

201

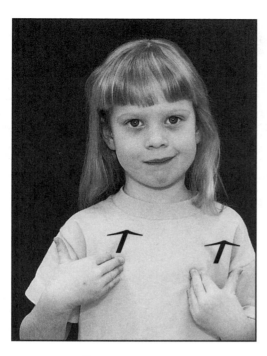

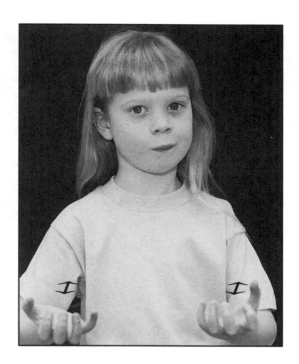

have

hands are bent about six inches out from the chest - move towards and touch chest once (used when you possess something, not as in "have to")

want

with flat hand palms up curve fingers several times (as if squeezing a ball several times)

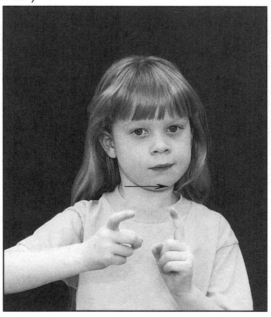

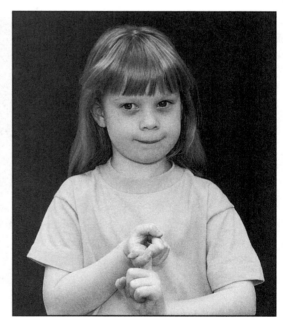

friend

with both x-shaped hands hook the fingers together (as if friends are hooked together)
variation two: with both x-shaped hands hook the fingers together then unhook and rotate hands and hook fingers together again

but / different

cross index fingers and move apart palm down in a slight arc
same sign for both, depends on context

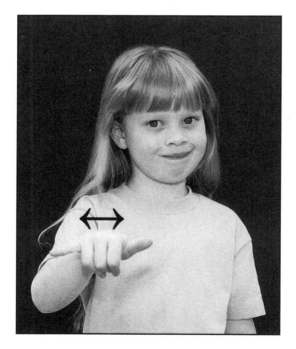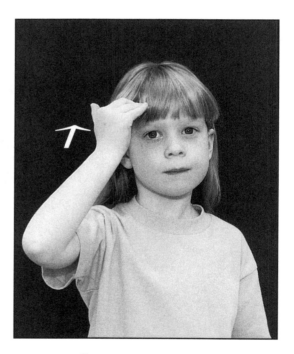

same/alike

with y-shaped hand move it sideways
several times a few inches each way
(as if the item on the left was the same
as the item on the right)

know

with bent-hand shape move towards
and touch the forehead on the right
once

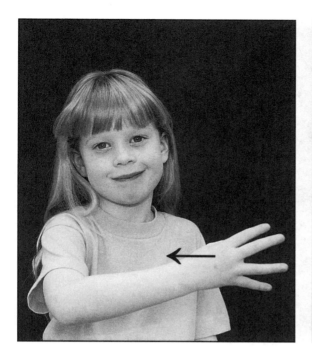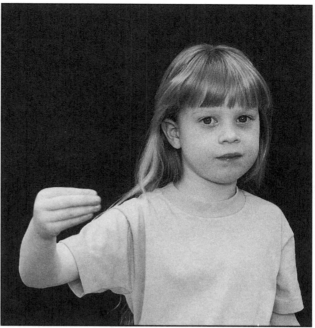

and

using a five-shaped hand with palm facing the left move hand left to right while closing the fingers together until they all touch into a flat-o shaped hand

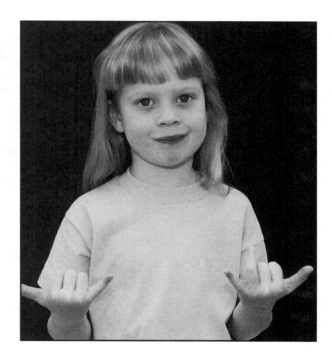

bed

plams together placed on side of head
(as if head was resting on a pillow)
variation two: use only one hand

now

with two y-shaped hands, palms facing
up move hands down once and firmly
(as if conveying "right now")

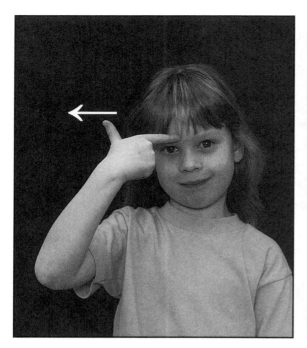 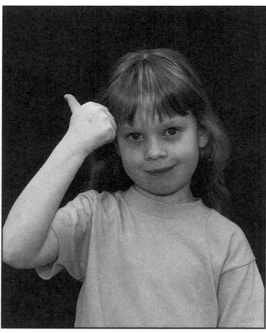

because

with index finger on forehead and thumb up move index finger into hand to
form the ten-shaped hand while moving hand away from head a few inches
variation two: sign the same way as forget

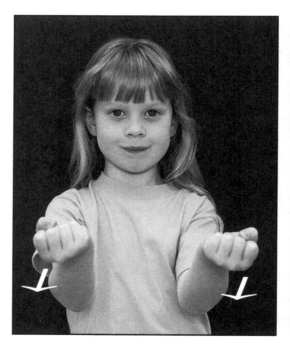 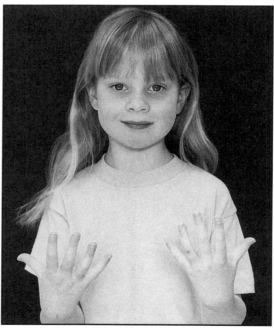

many

with s-shaped hands open hands and move outward
(similar to how many but the hands move outward not upward)

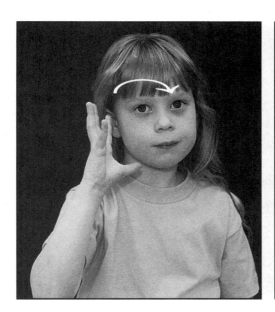

pretty

use 5-shaped hand on the side of the face and move in front of the face
in an arc from right to left when reaching the left side of the face the hand
becomes an o-shaped hand

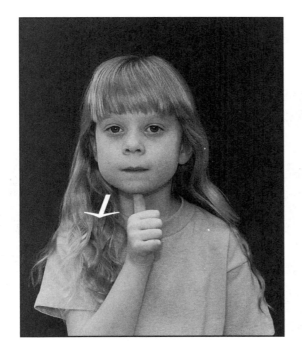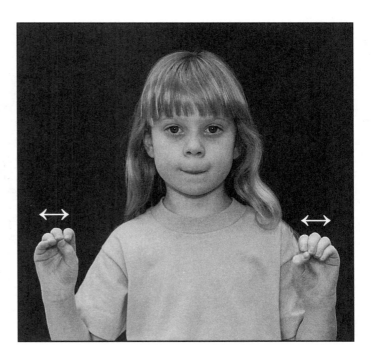

not

ten-shaped hand under chin with
thumb touching chin move thumb
outward with a slight arc downward

nothing

with o-shaped hands move hands back and
forth slightly several times

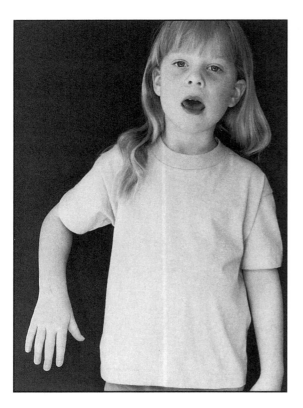

not yet

with mouth open and open-hand shape by the waist with palm facing towards your back move hand backwards two times

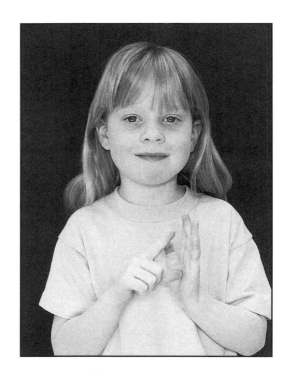

later

with the left hand out palm facing right place the thumb of the L-shaped hand on the left palm and move the hand downward in a circular arc while keeping the thumb in place on the left hand

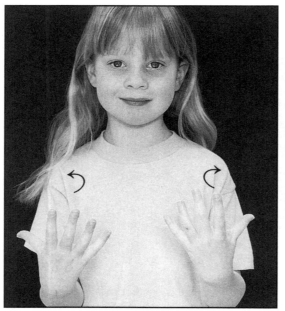

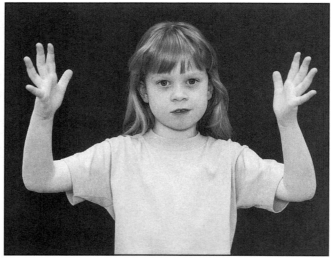

finished

with both hands up in front of the chest in the 5-shape and palms facing inward twist both hands outward once (as if conveying "finally done")

Getting Started with Sentences

ASL	English
ME HAPPY	I am happy.
HE HAPPY	He is happy.
SHE HAPPY	She is happy.
WE HAPPY	We are happy.
THEY HAPPY	They are happy.
YOU HAPPY	You are happy.
IT HAPPY	It is happy.
MOM HAPPY	Mom is happy.
DAD HAPPY	Dad is happy.
GIRL HAPPY	The girl is happy.
BOY HAPPY	The boy is happy.
FRIEND HAPPY	The friend is happy.

Now replace HAPPY with the other signs from each chapter.

Example:

ASL	English
ME SAD	I am sad.
HE SAD	He is sad.
ME HOT	I am hot.
HE HOT	He is hot.
DAD HOT	Dad is hot.
MOM COLD	Mom is cold.
SHE COLD	She is cold.
TODAY COLD	Today is cold.
NOW COLD	Now it is cold.
THERE COLD	It is cold over there.

(Note: There is no "to be" verb [is, are, was, were, be, am] in ASL same as some other foreign languages)

Question Forms

Now we can use the signs in various other sentences. Remember, questions are formed with the signs and the face. The eyebrows are moved up for a yes/no question and moved down for a question using a WH FORM (who, what, where, why, when, which, how, how many, how much). If the eyebrows are not moved up or down then the signs become a statement of fact, not a question. Also in asking a question, you move your head forward slightly and have a questioning look on your face.

Eyebrows down

SAD WHY	Why are you sad?
SAD WHO	Who is sad?
SAD WHAT	What is sad?
SAD YOU WHEN	When were you sad?

GIRL SAD WHERE	Where is the sad girl?
SAD HAPPY WHICH	Which are you, happy or sad?

Eyebrows up

SAD YOU	Are you sad?
SAD THEY	Are they sad?
SAD ME	Am I sad?
SAD WE	Are we sad?
SAD MOM	Is mom sad?
SAD IT	Is it sad?
SAD GIRL	Is the girl sad?
ME	Me?
YOU	You?
THEY	They?
US	Us?
HE	He?
MOM	Mom?

Remember: Questions that end with a yes or no response are called YES/NO Questions and require the eyebrows to be up.

Replace other signs you have learned in the questions to practice with all the signs from this book.

Negative Statements

When signing a negative statement the head is shaking back and forth as if gesturing no while signing the statement. Shake your head no while signing the underlined signs. Also furrowed eyebrows helps. Negatives signs are no, not and none.

YOU NOT HOT	You are not hot.
NO	No
HOT NONE	None are hot.
YOU	Not you.
ME EAT	I have not yet eaten.

If you signed the previous sentence while nodding your head yes, instead of no the sentence would mean the opposite, *I have eaten.*

Description signs (adjectives)

As in Spanish and many other languages, the adjective is used after the noun. In English you would say the   *The white car is ...*
In ASL you would sign   *CAR WHITE*

NIGHT HOT NOW	The night is hot now.
IX-BOY TALL CLEAN	The tall boy is clean.

Getting Started with Sentences

IX is the abbreviation for pointing toward something or someone. So in the above sentence point toward the boy and then sign boy.

In sentences where the adjective is at the end of the english sentence such as *The boy is clean*, the same is true in ASL.   *IX-BOY CLEAN*

Topic of the Sentence
Usually the most important item is signed first as a **topic** of the sentence. The sign is stressed using a forward movement of the head and maybe a slight movement of the body forward.

Example: **MY** CAR BROKEN
It is **my** car that is broken.

IX-CAR MY BROKEN
That car is mine and it is broken.

BROKEN MY CAR.
Broken, is the state of my car.

Other Grammatical Structures
There are other sentence structures in ASL which you can learn after you get the basics down. Check your local library for other reference materials.

More signs in a sentence or phrase

ASL	English
MORE MILK PLEASE	More milk please.
CARS FIVE RED	Five red cars
PIG DIRTY	The pig is dirty.
WATER GREEN COLD	The water is green and cold.
IWANT FRENCH FRIES	I want french fries.
I WANT HAMBURGER FOR LUNCH	I want a hamburger for lunch.
GIRAFFE AND ELEPHANT TALL	The giraffe and elephant are tall.
PHONE ON TABLE	The phone is on the table.
HAT RED WHITE AND BLUE	The hat is red, white and blue.
MY MOM AND DAD LOVE EAT ICE CREAM	My mom and dad love to eat ice cream.

Pop Quiz:

Find the English meaning of these signs in this book.

Hint: the first sign is a question word.

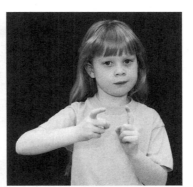

After playing this game, pick other signs and test yourself or have a friend test you.

Try guessing all the animals signs for example.

(How do you sign?)
Answer: HOW SIGNS

210

Getting Started with Sentences

English	ASL
The water is hot.	WATER HOT
The water is cold.	WATER COLD
The pizza is hot.	PIZZA HOT
The pizza is cold.	PIZZA COLD
The iron is hot.	IRON HOT
The oven is hot.	OVEN HOT
The food is hot.	FOOD HOT
The doll is dirty.	DOLL DIRTY
The doll is clean.	DOLL CLEAN
The spoon is dirty.	SPOON DIRTY
The sppon is clean.	SPOON CLEAN
The red ball is big.	BALL RED BIG
The pink car is little.	CAR PINK LITTLE
I love rabbits.	ME LOVE RABBIT
I like rabbits.	ME LIKE RABBIT
I love books.	ME LOVE BOOK
I like flowers.	ME LIKE FLOWER
I like candy.	ME LIKE CANDY
Where is the hat?	HAT WHERE [WHQ]
Where is the animal?	ANIMAL WHERE
Where is the 5?	5 WHERE [WHQ]
The shoe is in the box.	SHOE IN BOX
The candy is in the box.	CANDY IN BOX
The balloon is in the box.	BALLOON IN BOX
I want 2 napkins.	ME WANT NAPKINS 2
Two more please.	TWO MORE PLEASE
Time for lunch.	TIME FOR LUNCH
Who likes salad?	LIKE SALAD WHO [WHQ]
Who likes snakes?	LIKE SNAKE WHO [WHQ]
The dress is on the table.	DRESS ON TABLE
What time is it?	TIME WHAT [WHQ]
The sock is wet.	SOCK WET
The umbrella is wet.	UMBRELLA WET
Ice is cold.	ICE COLD
Icecream is cold.	ICE CREAM COLD
The book is sad.	BOOK SAD
The girl is sad.	GIRL SAD

English	ASL
The girl is happy.	GIRL HAPPY
The boy is happy.	BOY HAPPY
The boy is sad.	BOY SAD
Is your name Nicole?	NAME YOUR NICOLE [Y/NQ]
Do you live in Fresno?	YOU LIVE FRESNO [Y/NQ]
Is your house green?	YOUR HOUSE GREEN [Y/NQ]

WHQ: WH Question format - eyebrows down

Y/NQ: Yes/No Question format - eyebrows up

Index

Notes

Notes

Notes

Notes

Notes

Notes

Notes

Notes

Notes

Notes